SCIENTIF

QUEEN = REARING,

——AS——

PRACTICALLY APPLIED,

——BEING A——

METHOD BY WHICH THE BEST OF QUEEN-BEES ARE
REARED IN PERFECT ACCORD WITH
NATURE'S WAYS,

——BY——

G. M. DOOLITTLE.

FOR THE AMATEUR AND VETERAN IN BEE-KEEPING.

THIRD EDITION — FOURTH THOUSAND.

CHICAGO, ILL.
GEORGE W. YORK & COMPANY,
Publishers American Bee Journal,
144 & 146 Erie Street.
1901.

Scientific Queen Rearing by G.M. Doolittle

2010 reprint

© Northern Bee Books

ISBN 978-1-904846-61-1

Published by

Northern Bee Books,

Scout Bottom Farm,

Mytholmroyd,

West Yorkshire HX7 5JS

Tel: 01422 882751

Fax: 01422 886157

www.GroovyCart.co.uk/beebooks

Printed by Lightning Source UK

THIS BOOK

IS AFFECTIONATELY DEDICATED
TO

Elisha Gallup,

MY TEACHER IN BEE-KEEPING,

From whom I learned my first lessons in Queen-Rearing, and who truth-
fully claimed that around the Queen centers all
there is in Apiculture.

Northern Bee Books

INDEX TO CHAPTERS.

INDEX TO COMB HONEY MANAGEMENT.

INDEX TO ILLUSTRATIONS.

PREFACE.

For many years I have been urged to write a book on bee-keeping, and almost scolded because I did not do so. My excuse for not doing so has been, that there were many exhaustive treatises on this subject already before the public, written by Messrs. Langstroth, Quinby, King, Cook, Root, and others —hence there was no reason for thrusting more books upon the world, which had nothing for their subject-matter but the general outlines of bee-keeping.

As all bee-keepers of to-day are aware, I have given all of my best thoughts, on the subject which the desired book would cover, free to the world through our many bee-papers, so, had I complied with the request made, the matter in the book would have been mainly that which I had written before ; and owing to this self-same cause, the reader will perhaps find some fault with the present work.

Finally, the urgent requests of my friends for a book became so numerous, that I decided to hold back from the public a part of my experiments and research along the line of queen-rearing (as in this branch of our pursuit I have taken more interest, and gave to it more thought and study than to all else pertaining to apiculture), and when that research and the experiments were completed, give all which I had dug out regarding queen-rearing to the public in book form. The culmination of this decision is now before you, and the reader can decide whether or not I have made a mistake in the undertaking.

Altho I have given to the book the title of " Scientific queen-rearing," there is much in it that is not scientific, as the reader will soon discover, and some lofty minds may pass it by in disdain on this account.

It is not a manual, giving in terse, sharp periods the greatest amount of accurate information in the briefest space. My style, I fear, is often like my bee-yard, which in looks is irregular, while it attempts something useful. I never could be pinned down to systematic work. I always did like to work at the bees near a gooseberry-bush, full of ripe, luscious fruit, or under a harvest apple-tree, where an occasional rest could be enjoyed, eating the apples which lay so temptingly about. Do we not all need an occasional relaxation from the severer duties of life? If so, the rearing of queens for our own apiary gives us a change from the all-important struggle for honey, whereby we can get money.

In brief, it is my sincere conviction that something to relieve the monotony of every-day life is good for humanity, and it is my wish to diffuse this belief as widely as possible.

I frankly admit that the following pages are very much the same in character as if I had taken the reader by the arm, from time to time, and strolled about the apiary and shop in the time of queen-rearing, and chatted in a familiar way on the topics suggested as we past along.

At the outset I shall undoubtedly be met by those inevitable " Yankee questions," Does queen-rearing pay ? Would it not pay me better to stick to honey-production and buy the few queens which I need as often as is required ?

I might answer, Does it pay to kiss your wife ? to look at anything beautiful ? to like a golden Italian Queen ? to eat apples or gooseberries ? or anything else agreeable to our nature ? is the gain in health, strength and happiness, which this form of recreation secures, to be judged by the dollar-and-cent standpoint of the world ?

Can the pleasure which comes to one while looking at a beautiful queen and her bees, which have been brought up to a high standpoint by their owner, be bought ? Is the flavor of the honey that you have produced, or the keen enjoyment that you have had in producing it, to be had in the market ?

In nothing more than in queen-rearing can we see the handiwork of Him who designed that we should be climbing up to the Celestial City rather than groveling here with a " muck-rake " in our hands (as in " Pilgrim's Progress) trying to rake in the pennies, to the neglect of that which is higher and more noble. There is something in working for better queens which is elevating, and will lead one out of self, if we will only study it along the many lines of improvement which it suggests. I do not believe that all of life should be spent in looking after the "almighty dollar ;" nor do I think that our first parents bustled out every morning with the expression seen on so many bee-keepers' faces, which seem to say, " Time is Money." The question, it seems to me, in regard to our pursuit in life, should not be altogether, "How much money is there in it ?" but, "Shall we enjoy a little bit of Paradise this side of Jordan ?"

However, being aware of the general indifference to Paradise on either side of Jordan, I will state that I have made queen-rearing pay in dollars and cents, having secured on an average about $500 a year therefrom for the past five years ; and that all may do as well, I proceed at once to describe the ground over which I have traveled, and tell how it is done.

Before doing so, however, I wish to say that all along the way I have pickt up a little here and there, so that most of the credit for that which is valuable in this book (if there is any value in it), belongs to some one else besides Doolittle. It has been pickt up in such little bits that I hardly know to whom I should give credit, so I will simply say, that most of the suggestions which I have received have come through the bee-periodicals, and quite largely from the reports which they have given of different thoughts dropt at many bee-conventions.

G. M. DOOLITTLE.

Onondaga Co., N. Y.,
        Christmas, 1888.

----------------✧----------------

Publishers' Note.

Upon informing Mr. Doolittle that the first edition of his book was about exhausted, hence a new one would soon be needed, and asking if any changes were necessary, the publishers received this answer thereto:

ONONDAGA CO., N. Y., Dec. 11, 1898.
GEORGE W. YORK & COMPANY,

   Dear Sirs :—Yours of the 9th at hand. Replying to your question, I would say that I do not think I care to re-write or revise any of the chapters in "Scientific Queen-Rearing," should a new edition be necessary. Later experience only proves the correctness of the position taken in 1889, when the first edition was publisht.

G. M. DOOLITTLE.

Queen-Bee (magnified) and Egg.

In Memoriam G. M. Doolittle.

Gilbert M. Doolittle died at his home near Boroclino, N. Y., on June 3, 1918, aged 72 years, 1 month and 19 days. Altho Mr Doolittle had suffered from serious ill health for a long time, his final illness was of the duration of only two days, death resulting from prostration due to the extreme heat of June 1 complicated with the results of contracting a severe cold. His whole long and useful life was spent on a farm in the immediate neighborhood of his birthplace. He was born the son of a farmer and beekeeper, and from his very infancy he was himself a beekeeper.

By the death of G. M. Doolittle, the voice of a great beekeeper-teacher has been stilled. For almost half a century he unceasingly taught the principles and details of good beekeeping thru the apicultural journals to a great audience of both beekeeper learners and beekeeper experts. Among all the correspondents of the bee journals no writer, perhaps, has been more closely followed than Mr. Doolittle. The readers of Gleanings thru many years have expressed in thousands of letters their appreciation of him as a teacher. So universally was his opinion sought that Gleanings Editor, early in 1900, asked him to conduct a department in Gleanings entitled "Conversations with Doolittle." In that capacity Mr. Doolittle has been a continuous instructor to the American beekeeping public for more than 18 years. He has been a regular contributor to this journal from the first year of its publication, 1873.

From his earliest years, Mr. Doolittle was a very close observer, and his statements as to the actual operations that take place within the hive (or what we now technically call bee behavior) can be regarded as authentic. He came to be generally accepted as an authority on all manner of domestic economy of the bees.

Mr. Doolittle was a large man in every way, of magnificent physique and commanding presence, the possessor of a fine voice, a ready and witty speaker, a good storyteller, and an excellent writer. In the telling of witty stories that illustrated valuable points in beekeeping, he surpassed any beekeeper we have ever known At the great Buffalo beekeeper's' convention in 1897, we recall that he was frequently called on, and each time he brought down the house with roar upon roar of laughter and applause. His stories always had a good point.

One of Mr. Doolittle's most emphatic teachings was that the beekeeper must follow nature - that no beekeeper could succeed if he did not follow nature's rules. One of his chief theorems was that good queen-cells must be reared in strong colonies built up to the swarming pitch, and, as a corollary of' this, he often said that good cells could not be built unless honey or sealed stores were supplied daily. He rightly and stoutly held that no queen-breeder could succeed unless he observed these two rules. He was first to prove that good cells could be built under only two impulses - the swarming impulse and the supersedure impulse. Good queen breeders now recognize these two propositions as fundamental.

Altho Doolittle did not invent artificial queen-cups, he was the first man to develop the process. His method of making artificial cell cups started a new era in queen rearing

While cell cups are now made in a wholesale way by machinery, the basic principle is Doolittle's. He was also the first man to demonstrate that queens can be reared in an upper story with a laying queen below. All in all, Doolittle's method of rearing queens is essentially those of all modern methods now in vogue, and this one contribution to beekeeping has done more to make better queens and consequently better colonies than any other one thing in beekeeping practice. His book on"Scientific Queen Rearing" is acknowledged today as containing the best of modern methods of queen-rearing.

Years ago Doolittle originated the slogan, 'rich in stores.' He talked it first, last, and all the time. He insisted that unless a colony at the beginning of the season had a great abundance of stores it would not build up as will a colony that has plenty of stores. Here again he was absolutely right, and was ever preaching this fundamental doctrine of good beekeeping. He developed a unique system of swarm control for the production of comb honey. This system is fully outlined in his book published under the title of "The Management of Out-apiaries."

Mr. Doolittle, while not original in the idea of melting wax by means of solar heat, was one of the first in this country to exploit the principle, and for years there has been on the market what was known as the Doolittle solar wax-extractor. He was one of the pioneers in the treatment of American foul brood. His ideas, away back in the early days, were entirely in harmony with those of Quinby, both of whom were absolutely right. During those days there were many false teachers and false teachings; but Doolittle's teaching and practice on the subject of foul brood during all that time were such as stand the test of present-day knowledge.

In the early days of the ABC of Bee Culture, Mr. Doolittle prepared, at A. 1. Root's suggestion, a series of comments showing wherein he differed from Mr. Root. The fact that the two men saw things so nearly alike was remarkable. That they differed in details was only natural. The fact that he was so nearly always right was because he spent hours and days studying his bees - because he learned at the hive.

One outstanding feature of Mr. Doolittle's beekeeping was that he was not only a good instructor, but he put his teachings into successful practice. Some men, like Langstroth, the peer of all instructors, never could make money from their bees. Others, like Quinby, one of the best authorities in his day, have made money, even with box hives. Doolittle always profited from his bees, and always succeeded in getting crops.

Mr. Doolittle was more than a successful beekeeper and natural-history student. He was a big-hearted friend, a good citizen, and a Christian gentleman.

Long will the good live after him that he has done. Peace to him!

Scientific Queen=Rearing.

CHAPTER I.

INTRODUCTORY REMARKS.

When I was about seven years old my father procured some bees by taking them of a neighbor on shares. I remember, almost as if it were yesterday, how animated I was, as he and the neighbor of whom he took the bees, came near the house with the hive suspended on a pole between them, by means of a sheet tied at the four corners. The hive was deposited on a bench a few rods from the back door of the house, one cold morning in early April, where it was thought that it would be a good place for them to take up their abode for the future.

My curiosity about these bees hardly knew any bounds, and altho that day was cold and dreary, I was often out by the hive to see if I could not catch a glimpse of some of the inmates. The first warm day on which they took a general flight, my delight was great to see them " cut up their antics " about the hive, as I termed it ; and when the first pollen appeared, or when they began to go into the hive with " yellow legs " (as father always would speak of the gathering of pollen, even in the later days of his life), I was near the hive an interested spectator.

As the days past by I became all anxiety about their swarming, and many were the questions which I plied father with in regard to how this was done. In answer to some of these questions, he told me that the queen led out the swarm, undoubtedly getting this impression from seeing the young queens of after-swarms out on the alighting-board with the first bees, when a second or third swarm issued. On the mention of the queen I wanted to know all about her, but it was very little that father could tell me, except that he often saw her with the swarm. As only box-hives were in use in this locality, it was no wonder that he knew so little regarding this all-important inmate of the hive, as now viewed from the present standpoint of our profession.

My anxiety for swarming-time to come was so great that it seemed that it never would arrive, and when it did come the impression which it made upon my mind was so lasting that, as I write, I can almost see those bees whirling and cutting circles in the air, seemingly thrice as large and active as is a swarm in my later years.

After they had clustered, were cut down, and brought to the empty hive, my anxiety to see the queen became paramount to all other interests which this exciting time presented; and when, as the last half of the swarm was going in, she was seen, altho only a brown German queen, I thought her very majestic in appearance, and the sight well worth all the hunting we had done to find her.

Time past on, and in a few years the apiary had grown so that swarming was quite frequent, and had somewhat lost its novelty; yet there has been no time in my life but what it has had very much of interest to me.

During one swarming season a third swarm issued, and in alighting it separated into three parts, so that none of the little clusters had more than a quart of bees, while one had scarcely more than a teacupful. Father was about to put all of the three clusters into one hive, but I finally persuaded him to let me put the little one into a small box that I had, and see what I could do with them. In getting them into the box I saw three queens go in, which excited my curiosity very much. I remember planning how such swarms, which had many queens, might be multiplied to great numbers; but to say that any idea of queen-rearing entered my head at this time would savor of imagination.

The little colony built three pieces of comb a little larger than the hand, but soon after cold weather came the bees died, as father had said they would, when he let me try the experiment. In a year or two more that dreaded disease—foul brood—appeared in the apiary, and as father knew nothing about how to control it, all the bees were soon gone.

Years went by with little or no interest on my part regarding bees, except as a runaway swarm past over my head while at work in the field, or as I and some of the neighboring boys robbed bumble-bees' nests; until at 17 years of age, in time of sugar-making, a bee-tree was found by hearing the roaring of bees on their cleansing flight, as I was going to visit a neighbor's sugar-bush not far away. The next warm day I went out looking for bees, and before noon I found another bee-tree. These trees were left until fall, when they were cut, but in falling they so scattered the bees and comb that with the little knowledge I then had I thought that I could not save them.

Twenty years ago I cut one of my feet so badly that I was confined to the house nearly all winter, and as reading was my chief amusement, it so chanced that I pickt up "King's Bee-Keepers' Text-Book," which I had purchast the year I found the bee-trees, because the advertisement about it said that it told "how to hunt bees." As soon as I began to read this book I contracted what is known as the "bee-fever," which took so strong a hold of me that I was not satisfied until I had borrowed and read Langstroth's book, and purchast Quinby's work, besides subscribing for the "American Bee Journal."

In the spring I purchast two colonies of bees, from which originated my present apiary. This was in the spring of 1869, and as that was a very poor season I secured only one swarm from the two colonies, and very little experience along any line of the pursuit, except that of buying sugar and feeding up these three colonies for winter.

The next June I went to see a man who kept some Italian bees (the first I had ever seen), who lived about four miles from me. When I arrived I found him at work at queen-rearing, so I was all interest at once. He showed me all that he knew of queen-rearing during my frequent calls on him that summer, and the next spring I went into partnership with him in the queen-business, he rearing the queens and I doing the selling—doing this by taking the queens around to the bee-keepers who lived within 10 or 15 miles of us, and introducing them into the apiaries of those who would buy. I remained in partnership with him during the next year, and, as a whole, I made it profitable, for I not only got some cash out of it, but at the end of that time I had a full knowledge of the old plans of queen-rearing. During this time I had partially Italianized my own apiary, so the next year I started out on "my own hook' in the queen-business, altho not doing much at it in the way of selling to outside parties till some years later.

After losing nearly, or quite, one-half of my queens, one spring, owing to their poorness in quality, I began to study up plans for the rearing of better ones, which study I have kept up till the present time. Into this branch of our pursuit I have put all the thought and energy at my command, as well as to apply the accumulated thoughts of others as exprest in our bee-papers, till I think that I can truly say there is much in the following chapters never before given to the public.

CHAPTER II.

IMPORTANCE OF GOOD QUEENS.

Upon no other one thing does the honey part of the apiary depend so much as it does upon the queen. Give me a good queen—one which can be brought up to the highest production of eggs, just when we want them—and I will show you a honey crop, if the flowers do not fail to secrete nectar; but with a poor queen—one that you must coax for eggs, to little or no purpose, at the right time—the flowers often bloom in vain, even when the honey-secretion is the greatest.

I have had in my apiary, at different times, queens that with all the coaxing which I could bring to bear on them during the forepart of the season, would not lay any more eggs previous to the honey harvest than were needed to keep the spring strength of the colony good, so that when the yield of honey was at its height there would not be one-fourth the number of bees to gather it that there should be. When the yield of honey came then these queens would begin breeding, so as to get plenty of bees in the hive just as the harvest closed, only to eat up the little honey that the few laborers there were in the harvest had gathered. The more queens of this sort a bee-keeper has the worse he is off. This is a peculiarity of the Syrian races of bees, but many poorly reared queens act in the same way, no matter to what race they belong.

Then, again, I have had queens which would not be coaxt to fill more than three or four Gallup frames with brood at any season of the year; so that at no time were there laborers enough in the hive to make a respectable showing, no matter how much honey there was in the field. Others would appear very prolific for a short time, but just when I wanted them the most, and when I supposed that all was going well, an examination would show that they had died of old age, even when they might not be more than six to twelve months old. This would cause a break in the production of bees at a time when every day of such production would count many pounds of honey in the honey harvest.

From the above it will be seen that in no one thing in bee-keeping does quality count for as much as it does with the queen or mother-bee. Of course, if we are only to count our colonies then a poor queen is better than none; and there are other times when she is such, as in holding a colony together till we can get a better one ; but I repeat, that an apiary with all poor queens is worse than no bees at all. When we come to fully realize the great achievements which can be obtained with a really good queen — one that will give us from 3,000 to 4,000 workers every day for a month previous to the honey harvest, we, as apiarists of America, will put forth more energy along this line of our pursuit than we ever yet have done.

Look at that colony you had one spring which gave you 100, 200, 400, 600, or even 1,000 pounds of honey (one or two reports of nearly 1,000 pounds of honey from a single colony have been given in the past, while the reports of those giving from 400 to 600 are numerous), and see why it did so well, while the average of your whole apiary did not come up to one-half that amount. Why did that colony do so well? Simply because it had a large working-force of the right age, and at the right time, to take advantage of the honey-flow when it came. And how came it to have such a force at the right time? Because the queen was a good one, doing her part just when she should, and not at some other time. Why did the others fail of doing the same thing? Either because they did not have good queens, or because the owner failed to have the queens do their duty, when they should have been doing it.

"But," says one, "can I get all colonies to do as well each year, as my best colonies do?" I will answer that by asking, What is there to hinder? If all are in the same condition as the successful one, would they not do equally well? Most assuredly they would. So then we see that the trouble lies in not having the colonies all equal with the one which did so well. The reason that all are not in the same condition devolves primarily upon the queen; and secondly upon the strength in which the colonies come through the winter. Of late, I have inclined to the opinion that on the queen rests, to quite an extent at least, much of the cause of our wintering troubles. One thing is certain, if we cannot have all colonies exactly alike, we can approximate very nearly to it—much nearer than many imagine, if we work for that object, along the line of bringing the queens to as nearly perfection as possible, and cease the breeding of cheap queens—that class which "do not cost the apiarist anything."

If there is anything in which I take some little pride it is that since I began to breed my queens for good quality, and for that only, this variation of yield of honey from different colonies has grown less and less, till, at the present time, the average yield of honey from each colony in the apiary is very nearly alike, while fifteen years ago some colonies would give 75 percent more honey than would others.

What a few of our best queen-breeders can do all can do, if they will only put the same interest into their work along this line ; and one of the objects of this book is to tell those who desire how they can, by careful attention to the rules laid down herein, become breeders of the best of queens, as such are of great importance to the amateur as well as the specialist.

CHAPTER III.

NATURE'S WAY OF REARING QUEENS.

The Creator of all things lookt over His work after He had finisht it, so. we are told, and pronounced it "GOOD ;" hence we could reasonably expect that at that time all things created by Him were of the highest type of perfection. He then told all animated nature to "multiply and replenish the earth." For this reason we find a disposition in our bees to swarm, and altho during the last century men have tried with great persistency to breed this disposition out, or make a hive which would accomplish the same thing, yet so far that disposition stands defiant toward all of these unnatural schemes, and just as some individual is ready to cry "Eureka," out comes a swarm, and all of our plans lay prostrate in the dust.

Many have been the reasons given to account for bees swarming, such as the hatred of an old queen toward the rival inmate of a queen-cell, which the bees had succeeded in getting, in spite of her frowns and anger; the hive being too small to hold the accumulated thousands of workers, insufficient ventilation, etc.; yet in my opinion none of these things ever caused a swarm to issue, in and of themselves, for everything in Nature is held obedient to the command of Him who controls the universe. And I rejoice that this is so, for I firmly believe that better results can be obtained where bees swarm than would be the case if we could breed out the swarming-trait.

A new swarm goes to work with an energy never possest by the bees at any other time (unless it is by the parent colony) immediately after its young queen gets to laying. This swarming-trait also produces queens of the highest type of perfection, not being equaled by any except those reared under one other of Nature's conditions, which will be spoken of at length in the next chapter. Many have been the claims made that queens reared by different methods are *just as good* as those reared under the swarming impulse; but I have yet to hear it claimed that queens so reared are any better than are those reared where the swarm issued under the conditions which Nature designed they should.

I am met here by the claim that many colonies of Italian bees swarm without any preparations for swarming being made, by way of providing queen-cells before the swarm issues, as is usually the case; and that queens reared under such circumstances—where there are but few bees in the hive to feed, nurse, and keep the royal occupants of the cells warm —certainly cannot be as good as those reared under the superior planning of the skilled apiarist.

I freely admit that queens reared by some of the plans of "artificial" queen-rearing, may excel such queens, but I claim that the first-named conditions are not such as Nature originally designed they should be. I do not believe that an isolated colony (as all colonies are isolated except by the intervention of man) ever cast a swarm under such conditions. It is the compacting of colonies together in large apiaries which brings about such results, thereby causing what is termed "the swarming-fever"—where swarms issue under the most unfavorable circumstances imaginable, sometimes even swarming without a queen, thus leaving the parent colony broodless, and without means from which to provide themselves with a queen. After careful watching in my own apiary for years, and closely questioning other bee-keepers, I have yet to find where the first swarm of the season, from any apiary, has ever issued previous to the sealing of the first queen-cell.

"But," says one, "you are always crying 'Nature! Nature!!' Don't you know that man's intelligence, by opposing Nature's laws at the right time, can get ahead of her ways, and thus secure better results?" No, I did not know any such thing; nor do I believe it. It is only as the intelligence of man moves along harmoniously with the laws of Nature that any improvement can be expected. Is not this true?

Suppose I cut my finger quite badly, and when it stops bleeding I wonder what I am to do with it to have it get well as quickly as possible. While I am thus wondering, along comes a man of superior (?) intelligence, and he says, "I see you have cut your finger. I am glad I happened along just at this time, for I have a salve which will heal up that wound at once, and, by your using it, your finger will be as well as ever

in a few days. This salve of mine has the greatest healing
properties of any salve known." Reader, do you believe that
the *salve* has any healing quality, or that my finger will ever
be as perfect as before ? I do not. All that any salve can claim
as doing, is to assist Nature to make the best of a bad job, for
it is Nature that does the healing, not the salve. Would I not
have been better off had I not cut the finger ?

Again, some day during the month of June, I chance to
run against the body of a choice apple-tree with the hub of
my wagon-wheel ; and in doing so I knockt a patch of bark
off the the tree as large as my hand. Along comes a man
familiar with grafting, and applies some grafting-wax, saying,
" This will heal over the place, and make it as good as ever."
Do you believe it ? Will not the tree always show a scar ? In
the knocking off of that bark the apple-tree received a shock,
or something which was contrary to its nature, and as soon as
the first effect was over every power that was in the tree was
brought to bear on this place to remedy the damage, and it
was only wherein the wax kept off the warring elements which
would work against the repairing of the damage, that the wax
did any good. Just so with anything that goes against Nature's laws. The first thing to be done is to get rid of the antagonizing force, and as soon as that is done Nature tries to
get back to the spot where she was before, as nearly as possible, and as quickly as she can.

Let a man take a drink of whisky, and in a little while
you will see him cutting up all manner of antics (that otherwise he would not have thought of doing), when you call him
" drunk." What is the matter ? He has taken something
into his system that is not moving harmoniously with Nature,
and Nature is trying to " kick " out this antagonizing force.
If so much antagonizing force (whisky) has been taken that
Nature has to kick vigorously to expel it, the man is kickt
over for the time being ; but after this force has been expelled
Nature begins the work of healing, and the man " rights " up
again, but never gets back to where he was before.

Now apply this to the bees : Along comes the antagonizing force—the apiarist—who is going to rear queens intelligently (unnaturally), and kills the mother of the colony.
What is the result ? The whole colony acts for the first few
hours very much as did the man after having drank the
whisky. What is the trouble ? Why, Nature is " kicking,"
that is all. After becoming reconciled to fate, the bees,
through Nature's law, go to work to repair the damage done,
and, as in all of the other cases, she does this as quickly as
possible, even where only eggs are given from which to rear a
queen. Under these conditions antagonizing forces come in,

and I do not believe that the "wound" can be made as good as ever, any more than they could in the three illustrations which I have used. Queens partially deficient in some points will be the result.

Some claim that this last is a natural condition for a colony of bees to be placed in, but I take exception to any such claim, for there are very few colonies that ever find themselves in such a condition without the interference of man. During all of the ages, up to within about a century past, how different the methods whereby queens were produced which have stood the test of thousands of years.

Let us look at Nature's plan for a moment or two, so as to see how it does compare with the above work of many of our apiarists. We find that queen-rearing and swarming are only done during a period when both honey and pollen are being gathered from the fields. When this condition of things prevails, the bees are getting strong in numbers, and soon embryo queen-cells are started, in which the queen lays the eggs which are to produce the royal occupants.

Some claim that it is not fully settled that the queen deposits the egg in the queen-cells at the time of natural swarming; but my assistant once saw her do it, and so have others, while the position of the eggs in the cells prove it, even had no one ever witnest her in the act. Others claim that the queen lays the eggs in worker-cells along the margin of the comb, when the bees build queen-cells over them. Any one familiar with the inside of a bee-hive, should know that such reasoning is fallacious, for the embryo queen-cells are often formed many days before eggs are found in them, as thousands of bee-keepers can testify.

These eggs remain in this form for about three days, when they hatch into larvæ which the bees now begin to feed. Some claim that royal jelly is placed around these eggs before they hatch, but if this is true it is something I have never seen, altho I have watcht this matter very closely for years. Neither do I find that the larvæ are fed much more plentifully during the first thirty-six hours of their existence than are larvæ in worker-cells; but when about this age the bees begin to feed them so liberally on royal food that they actually float in it during the rest of their growth; this supply often being so great that there is left a lump as large as a pea of partially dried food, after the queens emerge from their cells, while all of their operations are conducted leisurely, for the bees are in no haste for a queen, as their mother is still with them in the hive. There is no hurrying up to replace a loss, thereby using old larvæ, or scantily feeding the same as is done when Nature is antagonized; but all is done by a system reaching perfec-

tion. If a cold, bad time comes on now they do not hesitate
to tear down the cells and wait for a favorable time to come
again for them to " multiply and replenish the earth."

All of this shows us that the bees are only obeying the
laws which govern the economy of the hive, instead of a force
outside of that economy, which compels them to make good a
loss that man has brought about. It seems to me that we can
always consider it safe to go according to the teachings
learned by a close observation of our " pets," and unsafe to go
contrary to the rules and laws which govern them. At least
this is the belief which I have always had, and along this line
has been my study, while trying to find out the best plans
whereby queens of the highest type could be reared. I have
never succeeded in rearing queens which pleased me every
time till I commenced to work in harmony with Nature's
plans. When I learned so to work I found that my queens
were improving all the while, and to-day I am well satisfied
that I have made a great improvement iu my stock beyond
where it was ten years ago.

CHAPTER IV.

ANOTHER OF NATURE'S WAYS.

Besides what is known as the " swarming plan," the bees
have another way of rearing the best of queens, which, together with the former, are the only plans by which queens
are reared, except where the bees are forced to do so by some
abnormality of the colony. My experience goes to prove that
where such abnormality exists, queens which are then reared
do not come up to that high standard that they do where
reared as Nature designed they should be. However, there
are very few queens reared except when the colony is in a
normal condition, only as the colony is interfered with by man;
so that we find the usual plans adopted by nearly all queen-
rearers of the past, going in the direction of these few excep-
tions rather than along the line which Nature designed.

While rearing queens by the " forcing process " (at times
when they could not be reared by natural swarming), I came
across a colony in early spring, which had, as far as I
could see, a good queen, yet on the combs there were two very

nice queen-cells under way, with larvæ floating in an a' undance of royal jelly. As queen-cells which were formed in my queen-rearing colonies, when workt by the "forcing process," were not supplied in this fashion with royal jelly, I decided to keep watch of this colony and see if I could not learn something.

In due course of time these cells were sealed, when, to all outside appearances they were just as perfect as I had ever seen in natural swarming; while the cells which I was compelling the bees to build by taking their queens away from them did not so appear. One of the cells I transferred to a nucleus, just before it was ready to hatch, while the other was left where it was, to see what would become of the matter. The queens hatching from both cells proved to be every bit as good as any queens I ever reared in the height of the honey harvest by natural swarming, even altho it was by dint of coaxing that I could get queens reared at all by the "forcing" plans, as adopted fifteen years ago; while none of the "forced" queens would compare with these two in beauty, vigor, or length of life.

Soon after the young queen which was left in the old hive commenced laying, the old mother began to decline, and, in the course of a week or two was gone; yet had I not opened this hive for a month, at this time I would never have known that a change had taken place as regards the queen, from the appearance of the brood which was in the hive.

Right here let me say, that from all of my experience with bees, I am led to conclude that 999 queens out of every 1,000 reared, where man does not interfere with the bees, are reared by one of these two plans; yet there are those persons among our number who claim that they are along the line of Nature; or rearing queens by a still better plan than these two, where they take away the queen from a colony at any time they think best, and compel the bees to rear others, often when it would be the last thing the colony would wish to do. Gentlemen, your position is not a consistent one, nor is it one that you would adopt along any other line except queen-rearing; and I hope that this book will open your eyes, so that in the future you will try to be in accord with the wants of the bees, and thus be rearing queens of superior quality instead of those which cannot be other than inferior.

To return: After I had this experience with the colony that had "two queens in a hive" (which was a surprise to so many fifteen years ago, when it was thought that no colony ever tolerated but one laying queen at a time), I began to watch for a like circumstance to occur, which happened about a year from that time. In the latter case, as soon as I found the cells they were sealed over, and not knowing just when they would hatch, I at once cut them out and gave them to nuclei. In a few days I lookt in the hive again, when I found more cells started, which were again cut off and given to nuclei just before it was time for them to hatch. In this way I kept the bees from their desired object for some two months, or until I saw that the old queen was not going to live much longer, when I left one of the cells which they had under headway to mature. By this plan I got about sixty as fine queens as I ever reared, and laid the foundation for my present plan of securing queens, which is about to be given in this book.

As time past on I was always on the lookout for such cases of building queen-cells, with the old queen present in the hive, where there was no desire to swarm, and in this way I have secured hundreds of splendid queens with which to stock my own apiary, and to send to those who desired queens of the best grade. If there is any difference between queens reared by this last of Nature's ways and those reared by natural swarming, that difference is in favor of queens reared to replace the old mother, when she shall get past being of use to the colony; so that I have no hesitation in pronouncing, queens thus reared of the highest grade which it is possible for the intelligence of man, combined with the natural instinct of the bees, to produce.

Having decided that queens thus reared were superior to any other, the thing next to be done was to get some plan that the bees would accept, whereby queens could be so reared just when and where the apiarist desired. To accomplish this I have studied hard and workt faithfully, putting into it all of my best thought for some six years past, till I have perfected a plan whereby I rear queens by Nature's best method, in the same hive with a laying queen, and that, too, just when and where I wish to have them reared, having queens in a single colony in all stages of development, from the just-hatcht larvæ to virgin queens, and those just commencing to lay. All about how to do it will be told in this book, but, before doing so, I wish to take the readers over some of the ground which I have traveled, so that they can see some of the steps taken ; for, in thus seeing, perhaps some new thoughts may be suggested to them which will lead in other directions from what is here given, which, when followed out by some other person than myself, may be of great help to the bee-fraternity.

CHAPTER V.

OLD METHODS OF REARING QUEENS.

My first experiments at queen-rearing were tried in 1870. During the month of July a second swarm issued having two queens, and as I saw them on the alighting-board of the hive, the thought came to me that here was a chance to save a nice queen, which, when she got to laying, could be used to replace an old one that I had in the apiary. Accordingly, I detacht the alighting-board, as soon as I saw one of the queens go in, and took the board with all the adhering bees to another hive, in which I put an empty comb, hiving the little lot of bees and queen in it.

At night I read up on queen-rearing (as far as I could with the books which I then had), from which I found that the way to rear queens was to place little colonies in small or nucleus hives, they having frames from four to six inches square. As I wanted to do things as they should be done, I went to work the next morning and constructed a little hive that held three frames about five by six inches. Into these frames I fitted comb, then went to the hive containing the little swarm and shook them out of it into this small hive. In due course of time the queen commenced to lay, and was used as I had designed.

I then began to look up what I was next to do with the little colony, and found all that was necessary was, to leave them alone, when they would start two or three queen-cells, which would be well taken care of, and make just as good queens where but a small nucleus was used as would a larger number of cells in a full colony. Queen-rearing now lookt very simple and easy to me, so I left the nucleus to mainly care for itself for the next five days. From time to time, as I lookt into the little hive (for I was so anxious about the matter that I could not keep away from it), I expected to find queen-cells started, but every time I opened the little box not a cell could be found.

The fifth day after I took the queen away, a bee-keeper came along who was considered quite a queen-breeder in those days, and to him I told the story of my trial at queen-rearing. He askt to see the little colony, and when I showed it to him, he quietly cut a hole in one of the combs where the smallest larvæ were to be found, saying that "now they would start some cells," which they did. He also said that "while the most of the queens then reared were reared in just such little nucleus hives, yet he believed that it was better to rear them in full colonies, as he thought queens thus reared were better fed, and that the warmth of a full colony was conducive to a better development of the royal occupants of cells built, hence we secured more prolific and longer-lived queens."

In due time one of the cells hatcht in the nucleus, and the queen was so small and so poor that I decided if I must have such inferior queens as that I would let the bees do their own queen-rearing, as I had done in the past.

When the next season came I found myself again longing to "dabble" in queen-rearing, so at it I went, altho I never again tried the nucleus boxes in doing so; for when I came to look into the matter more thoroughly, I was convinced that the best nucleus that I could possibly have was one or two frames in an ordinary hive. In this way all work done by the nucleus was readily available for the use of any colony, after I was through with the nucleus.

In trying this the next time I simply took the queen away from the colony I wanted to breed from, at a time when there was plenty of honey and pollen in the fields, for by this time some were opposing the plan of rearing queens in nucleus boxes, and also claiming that the only proper time for rearing queens was when plenty of honey and pollen were to be had by the bees, as it was natural for the bees to rear queens only at such times. I succeeded in getting a fine lot of cells from which some extra-nice queens were obtained—as I then considered them.

This caused the queen-rearing "fever" to run high, which, together with my procuring some Italians, caused me to work at it many times during the summer, altho I determined not to spoil my prospects of a crop of honey by using too many colonies in the business. Altho using Italian bees for queen-rearing (as it was then claimed that black nurses would contaminate the young queens), yet during this summer I succeeded in getting as high as 157 queen-cells built on one comb, while the usual number built by one colony would be only from three to twenty on all of the combs in a hive. If I could have had the Syrian bees at that time the number of cells might not have been so much of a wonderment to me. I thought this a great achievement, and something well worth being proud of, so I told my neighbors about it, and gave it to some of the bee-papers also.

All went on "swimmingly" until the spring of 1873, when, without any cause as far as I could see, one-half of all the queens that I had in the apiary died, leaving the apiary in poor condition for the honey season, which caused me to meditate a little on what could be the reason for such a wholesale death of my beautiful queens. A careful looking into the matter revealed that of all the queens that had died two-thirds were those which had been reared the previous season, while not one had died from those that had been reared by natural swarming.

What seems strange to me now, in looking back over the past, is, that all of these queens died so suddenly, and the bees made no effort at superseding them. They all had brood in abundance for the time of year, and the first I knew that all was not right was when I would find them dead at the entrances of the hives. After this I began to try other plans of queen-rearing, none of which pleased me any better than the one I had been using.

About this time there came a general dissatisfaction with most of the plans then termed "artificial queen-rearing," and the reason given for queens so reared not living any longer, or doing any better, was that such queens were not reared from the egg for a queen, but were fed worker-food for a time, and queen-food afterward, thus producing a bee that was part worker and part queen; hence, it could not be as good as a bee that was a perfect queen in all her parts.

Then came the following process, which I often see given at the present time, as one by which prolific and long-lived queens can be obtained:

Take a frame of new comb and put it in the colony having the breeding queen, leave it there till you see the first larva hatcht, when it is to be taken out, the bees shaken off, and then placed in an empty hive that is to be put on a stand of a populous colony, after moving the colony away. This is to be done in the middle of the day, when plenty of bees are flying.

After trying this method of procedure a few times, I came to the conclusion that it was one of the very poorest ever given to the public; for the queens so reared were very nearly, if not quite, as inferior as were those reared in the little nucleus boxes.

And how could it well be otherwise? For by such a plan only field-bees were obtained as nurses, while Nature designed young bees to do this work. While in early spring old bees do nurse brood by their being brought up gradually to it, yet in this case bees that had gone out in search of honey, with no idea of ever again being called upon to nurse brood, and with a good mother in the hive when they left, were suddenly confronted with starving larvæ from which they must rear a queen at once, while chyme or royal jelly was the most remote thing which their stomachs contained. This is one of the many plans which go almost in direct opposition to Nature's laws, and one that I claim should never be used, if we want to have our bees improving instead of retrograding.

I might give many other ways by which good queens are

said to be reared, which are as inconsistent with the best quality in queens as darkness is when compared with daylight; but I forbear. I have gone over this ground of the past only to show how queens used to be reared, and how some bee-keepers still rear them, so shat those who read the methods soon to be given may compare them with those formerly used, and see how we have been advancing along this line of our pursuit. I wish to say to any reader of this book who is still practicing any of the old, poor plans, Don't do it any longer; for you must know, it seems to me, that only inferior stock can result from the longer continuation of such practice.

CHAPTER VI.

LATER METHODS OF REARING QUEENS.

After testing all of the then known plans, as given in the previous chapter, and becoming disgusted with them, I turned my attention toward natural swarming, as a means by which to rear queens in the future. Looking toward the end of getting as many queens from this source as possible, I began stimulating my best queen-rearing colonies early in the spring, by some of the many methods given to. accomplish this work, so as to get them to swarm early, and then by hiving the new swarms from these colonies, on frames of brood, kept them swarming till late in the season, so that, as a rue, I coulld get, in this wa y, all of the queens that I wisht to use in my own apiary.

If, at any time, I was likely to fail of this, I would take a piece of comb containing larvæ from my best queen, and after shaving the cells down to one-eighth of an inch of the septum of the cell, with a thin, sharp knife, so that I could see the larvæ plainly, I would go to a hive having an inferior queen, that was preparing to swarm, and after removing the larvæ from the queen-cells that they had under way, I would, by means of a goose-quill toothpick, having its point broad and curved [Fig. 1, see page 25], lift the larvæ from the piece of comb I brought, and put them down in the royal jelly which the larvæ from the inferior queen was enjoying only a few moments before. Some take a frame (brood, bees and all) from the hive having their best queen, and, when ready, lift the larvæ from the bottom of full-depth cells, but it bothers me to see to do this. Where it can be done, it saves cutting and otherwise injuring the combs, while the bees protect the larvæ from being chilled, should the day be cool. The cells thus operated upon were markt, by pushing 1½-inch wire-nails through the comb near them, so that if the bees constructed other cells, I would not be deceived.

In this work I often found partly-built queen-cells with nothing in them, or perhaps some would contain eggs, which, when I found them, I would take out, substituting the larvæ in their places. As a rule, I would be successful with these, as well as with those that were put into the cells that con-

Fig. 1.—Toothpick for Transferring Larvæ.

tained royal jelly, but now and then a case would occur when only those placed in royal jelly would be used.

Right here I wish to say, that only the best of tested queens should be used as queen-mothers—queens known to possess all the desirable requisites that make a good queen; and, as we must often cut the combs, to get the larvæ for transferring, it is better to have the poorest combs in the hives with these queens, so as not to spoil the good combs in the apiary; or, if preferred, we can keep these best queens in a very small colony, so that the bees will fill the holes made in the combs when taking out brood, by building in worker-comb, as such colonies always will do, if fed sufficient for this purpose. By thus working I obtained good queens, altho it required much work, and probably I should never have workt out other plans, had it not been that at about this time I began to have calls for queens, from abroad.

This placed me in a position where I must have some other process of queen-rearing, or refuse to take orders for queens. As I wisht to please all who desired some of my queens, I began experimenting, and soon brought out the following method, which I will give at length, as I still have to rear some queens by it early in the spring and late in the fall, when there are not enough bees in the hive, or when they are too inactive to use the new plan to be given in the next chapter. However, I use wax-cups (having royal jelly placed in them), as described later on, instead of embryo queen-cells, as will be spoken of here.

In changing larvæ from worker-cells to queen-cells, as

given above, the thought occurred to me, that if the bees would take the larva when put into a perfectly dry queen-cell, on the combs of a colony preparing to swarm, they ought to do the same when placed in a like condition in a queenless colony.

Previous to this, I had often changed larvæ in queen-cells started in a queenless colony, taking out those that the bees were nursing, and substituting others from my best queen, where the bees had plenty of royal jelly in the cells, and secured good queens by this plan, which is now used by very many of our best queen-breeders. Good queens are reared in this way, but the point about it that I do not like is, that the number of cells which will be started is very uncertain, while they are scattered about in different parts of the hive ; and worse than all, the combs have to be badly mutilated in cutting out the cells, or else much time spent at the queen-nursery, watching for the queens to hatch ; for, if this is not done, many of them will be destroyed.

But, how should I get the embryo queen-cells, in which to put the larvæ ? was the first thought which confronted me. I remember that away back in some of the bee-papers, some one had proposed making queen cells to order, on a stick, for a penny apiece, and why could I not so make them ? It would do no harm to try, I thought; therefore I made a stick, so that it would just fit inside of a queen-cell, from which a queen had hatcht, and by warming a piece of wax in my hand I could mould it around the stick, so as to make a very presentable queen-cup. While doing this, some one happened along, who wisht to see some of my queens, so I went out in the apiary to show them. In doing this, I noticed some queen-

Fig. 2.—Embryo Queen-Cup or Queen-Cell.

cups [see Fig. 2] which had just been started by the bees, and it was not long before I saw where the embryo queen-cells could be procured in plenty, if I saved all I came across in my manipulations with the bees. When I returned to the shop, I had about a dozen of these cups, that I had clipt off the combs, while showing my friend the queens, which, with the five or six artificial cells that I had made, gave me plenty for a trial.

To fasten these to the combs, I melted some wax in a little dish, over a lamp, when, by dipping the base of the queen-cups in the wax, and immediately placing the cup on the comb, it was a fixture. So as not to spoil a good comb, I took an old one, such an one as had been damaged by mice, or one that had many drone-cells in it; and to have the cells built in the center of the comb, as I wisht them, a piece was cut out as large as a man's hand, at the desired place. I now turned the comb bottom side up, and fastened as many queen-cups as I wisht queen cells built, along the now under side of the hole

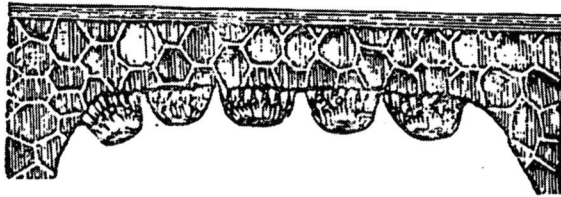

Fig. 3.—Comb with Queen-Cups.

that I had cut, and, after having transferred a larva into each cup, the comb was returned to its former position. [See Fig. 3.]

After taking the queen and all of the brood away from a populous colony, I substituted this prepared frame for the queen and brood. Upon looking the next day, to see what the result was, I found that the bees had destroyed all the larvæ but one, and that was in one of the cups that I had taken out of a colony.

Before I forget it, I will here say, that in all of my efforts at this time, to get the bees to use any of the cells that were made from beeswax, I made an entire failure; for, out of hundreds tried, not a larva could I get accepted, even when I gave a colony none other save cups thus made. However, later on I learned how to make the bees use them, as will soon be given. Not being willing to keep a colony queenless for one queen-cell, I gave back their brood and queen; then I sat down to study out the reason why I had made a failure.

The result of this study convinced me that no colony would immediately go to rearing queens after the old queen had been taken away from them. At the expiration of three days from the time the queen is taken away from a colony, the bees usually have numerous queen-cells under way, but rarely before; while in the above case, I had expected the bees to start them at once.

I now went to another populous colony and took its queen away, together with one comb, when a division-board feeder was placed where the comb was taken out. At night I fed the colony a little warm syrup (as they were not getting much honey at the time), and continued this nightly feeding for eight days.

Three days after taking the queen out, I went to the hive and took all of the brood away, but left the other combs having honey and food, arranging them close up to the feeder, leaving a place between the two central combs, for the prepared frame to be inserted. The hive was now closed, when the bees were shaken off the combs of brood, and the brood given to a colony which would care for it. On these combs were numerous queen-cells, which showed that the bees were

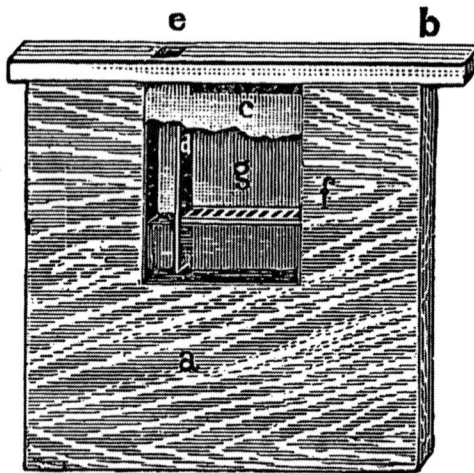

Fig. 4.—The Division-Board Feeder.

secreting or producing an abundance of royal jelly. As I wisht this jelly to accumulate in the stomachs of the nurse-bees, I took the brood away from them this time, before I put the larvæ into the queen-cups. In this way a colony will be prepared to rear as good queens as can possibly be reared, when no queen is present in the hive while the cells are being built, and is ahead of any other way that I ever tried, where the queen is to be taken away.

It will be seen that an hour before they were feeding thousands of working-larvæ besides the queen-larvæ, when, all at once, they are obliged to hold the accumulating chyme, and feel a great anxiety for a queen, as will be shown by their running all over the hive, flying in the air, and otherwise telling of their distrest condition, when you come with the prepared frame to put it in the hive. By now supplying them with from twelve to fifteen larvæ, all cradled in queen-cells, upon which they may bestow all the provisions and caresses that they were bestowing before on a whole colony, it could hardly result otherwise than in producing as good queens as could be produced by any plan not exactly in accord with Nature's ways.

On placing the frame in the hive, on this my second trial, I had great confidence of success, while the next day on opening the hive I was assured of it, by seeing all of the queen-cells accepted, except those that I had made of beeswax. These accepted cells were completed in due time, and from them I obtained queens which were as good mothers as any I had ever had up to this time, outside of queens reared by natural swarming. I now used this plan for many years, and if properly done, it never fails of giving fairly good queens. At all times when honey is not coming in abundantly, feeding is resorted to, and when the mercury is lower than 85° in the shade, all operations with the larvæ are done in a room of that degree of temperature, or a little higher.

But I think that I hear some one ask, " How old a larva do you use ? and, how about the occupant of a cell being fed royal food, from the time it is hatcht from the egg ?" I have conducted many experiments to see how old a larva may be, before being placed in the royal cell, and yet have it produce a good queen. Some who advocate that queens should be reared from the egg, claim that, in natural swarming, royal jelly is deposited around the egg before it hatches, so that the larva literally swims in jelly from that time until after the cell is sealed up ; and also that where an egg or larvæ is selected, from which to rear a queen in a queenless colony, adjoining cells are torn down, so as to make room for a large amount of royal jelly at the start.

I have carefully watcht, time and time again, to find out if an egg laid in a queen-cell was treated any differently for the first four days (after it was deposited in such cell by a queen), than an egg laid in a worker-cell, and as yet I have failed to find any difference ; so if any bee-keepers have seen what is described above, they have seen something that I have never been able to discover.

I also find, that where a colony is made queenless, the larva is floated out with royal jelly, till near the end of the cell, when a queen-cell is built out and downward over the comb, rather than that the bees tear away cells, as described ; especially is this the case with old combs.

At this time of hatching, the nurse-bees begin to feed the larvæ ; but, so far as I am able to judge, the larva in a worker-cell is surrounded by three times the food it can use, for the first thirty-six hours of its existence. Somewhere from this, to the time the larvæ are three days old, the bees begin to

stint them as to food, so that the organs are not developt as
they would be if fed abundantly during the rest of their larval
period.

I also claim that the food fed to all larvæ, up to the time
they are thirty-six hours old, is exactly the same, whether the
larvæ are designed for drones, queens, or workers ; and that the
difference comes by the queen-larva being fed large quantities
of this food, all of its larval life, while the others are fed sparingly later on, or else a different kind of food given after they
are thirty-six hours old. Some experiments which I have conducted point in this direction, but as yet I have not completed
them fully enough to warrant the giving of them here.

If the above is correct (and I firmly believe that it is) it
will be seen that the larva in a worker-cell has all of its wants
supplied for the first day and a half, and is developing towards
a queen just as fast, prior to this, in a worker-cell, as it possibly could in a queen-cell, surrounded by ten times the food
that it can consume.

Hundreds of experiments in using larvæ from three hours
old, up to those of thirty-six hours, prove that queens
from the former are in no way superior to those from the
latter, while the bees always choose the latter, where
the power of choice is left to them. As all of my plans of
rearing queens require the changing of small larvæ, I have
dwelt thus largely upon this very important point, so that the
reader might know just where I stand in this matter. Years
of success in producing the best of queens, together with the
result of many experiments, conducted by some of our
best queen-breeders, go to prove that I am correct in the above
conclusion.

A little practice will enable any one to know about how
old the larvæ are, by glancing at them in the bottom of the
cells. Bear in mind that a larva but thirty-six hours old is a
small affair, as the rapid growth is made at the latter end of
its life; and if you think that there is any chance of a mistake on your part, in not knowing larvæ of that age, or
younger, you should put a frame in a hive and watch for eggs,
then watch for the eggs to hatch into larvæ, when, by looking
in the cells from twenty-four to thirty-six hours afterward,
you will know to a certainty, just how such as you should use
will look. If you have been as correct as to the age of larvæ
used, as you should be, all of the queens will hatch from the
prepared cells, in from eleven-and-a-half to twelve days from
the time the frame was given to the queenless colony. An ex-
pert can judge so closely that he can figure the time of hatching to within three or four hours.

In taking care of these cells, I generally do it on the afternoon of the tenth day, if it is pleasant; for if deferred till the eleventh day it necessitates taking care of them on that day, no matter what the weather may be.

As soon as the cells are taken from the hive, I go to the colony which had the brood given them (when it was taken from this colony in preparing it for queen-rearing), and take three frames well filled with brood, on one of which is the queen, and place them back in the now queenless and brood-less hive, being particular to see, in putting the frames of brood in the hive, that the queen is on the center comb, so that the bees which go with her will surround and protect her, till all the bees become thoroughly mixt.

If it is early spring, I shake the bees in front of their own hive, from off the combs which do not have the queen on, so as to keep this colony as strong as possible; for in three days from this time, this colony is to go through the same course that the other did, in rearing more queens.

At the end of three days, all the brood that was left, is to be carried to the hive which now has the queen, so it will be seen that no colony will lose over thirteen days of time, by this process of queen-rearing, before it is back in nearly as good condition as ever. If we wish to save still more time to this colony, some colony can be kept purposely to care for the cells by keeping it queenless and giving brood occasionally to keep up the population. Into this colony the frames of queen-cells can be placed as soon as sealed, thus keeping none of the queen-rearing colonies queenless for more than eight days.

Some tell us that a queenless colony will rear four or five lots of queen-cells before the young bees get too old to rear perfect queens; but I say, do not rear but one lot of cells from any colony, at one time, if you wish to have good queens.

The reason is obvious, why a second lot of cells will not be as good, if you will take pains to read over what was said about getting the colony in condition to rear good queens. It would be nearly as bad as causing all old or field bees to rear queens, for the nurses have now been six days without anything that should cause them to prepare chyme, hence they have none in their stomachs to feed the laavæ, so they must go to work to produce more before they can do this work. By the time they could give them chyme, the larvæ would receive a check from which they would never recover, even if they could be fed as much and as good food afterward, which is unreasonable to suppose.

Since I adopted the above method, what is known as tne "Alley plan of queen-rearing" has been given to the public; but after a thorough trial, I fail to find any point wherein it is superior to the one given above, while in some few points I consider it inferior.

However, good queens can be reared by the Alley process —very much better ones than those reared by any of the old plans that were used by most of the queen-breeders before he gave his to the world. For this reason, Mr. Alley should have a prominent place assigned him, among the ranks of those who have done much to advance the cause of apiculture during the Nineteenth Century.

CHAPTER VII.

THE NEW WAY OF REARING QUEENS.

While rearing queens, as given in the last chapter, I became anxious for some plan by which I could get queens reared by natural swarming, so that the cells would be all on one comb, and in shape to care for as easily as were those which were built from the queen-cups that I gave to queenless colonies. For years I had practiced taking the larvæ out of queen-cells, which the bees had under way, and substituting larvæ from my best queen, by the transposition process; but in all of these cases I had to take up with the cells where the bees had built them, besides, in many instances, after going over all of the combs in a hive I would find only three or four cells, so I had to do a great deal of work without receiving much benefit from it; while in cutting off the cells, I was obliged to mutilate many of my very best combs. This did not please me, so I set about seeing what could be done by way of having cells built where I desired them.

To this end, I prepared cells the same as I had done in giving them to queenless colonies, after which I placed the frame in a hive where the colony was preparing to swarm. I then waited two days, when I opened the hive, hoping that the bees had taken the larvæ which I had given; but in this I was disappointed, for every one of them had been removed, while, much to my surprise, I found that every cell but two contained an egg deposited therein by the queen. In this I gained a point, even if it was not just what I had been looking for.

I now watcht these cells, to see what would become of them, and found that they were treated the same as others are—the colony swarming on the sealing of the first cell. As these cells were brought to perfection, I was not long in comprehending that in this I had a plan that would give me the cells all on one comb, the same being reared by natural swarming, and by it I could secure at least twice the number that I had ever been able to obtain before. By getting the colonies, having the best queens, to swarm early, and keeping them at it as late in the season as possible, I could rear fully four times as many splendid queens by this process as before, besides having the cells in such shape that every one of them could be saved with very little trouble.

In this way I kept on until I found that I could not find sufficient embryo queen-cells to keep up with my now increasing calls for queens, hence I must manage in some way to increase the supply of these, or else go back to the old way of queen-rearing for a part of my supply. The latter I very much disliked to do, which led me to go over the ground of making cells again, as I had formerly done.

While thinking of this matter, it came to me—why not dip the cells, the same as my mother used to dip candles? This thought so waked me up, that I wondered at myself for not thinking of it before, and immediately I had some wax in a small dish, over a lamp, to melt. While this was melting, I hunted up the old stick that I used in forming the cells at my first trial, which was nothing more than a tooth out of a common hand hay-rake. This tooth was now fitted to a queen-cup, as perfectly as I could do it with knife and sand-paper, while a mark was made around the tooth where the open end of the cell should come, so that I could know just how deep I wanted it to go in the wax, to give the desired depth of cell.

By this time the wax had melted. I then got a dish of cold water, and after dipping the end of the stick in the water (up to where it was markt, or a little deeper), and giving it a quick jerk, to throw off the water not needed, it was quickly lowered into the wax up to the mark, and as quickly lifted out, twirling it around and around in my fingers, so as to cause the wax to be equally distributed over the wood. I now had a film of wax over the stick, so frail that it could not be handled, but in it I saw the commencement of a queen-cell, which would, I was sure, be a boon to my fellow bee-keepers, for the wax much resembled the very outer edge of a queen-cup built on new comb.

I then dipt it again, not allowing it to go as deep within one-sixteenth of an inch as before, and in twirling the stick after taking it out, the end having the wax on was held lower than the other, so that the lower end, or the base, would be the thickest, as the wax would flow toward the lowest point.

As soon as the wax on the cell was cool enough to set, it was again dipt, not allowing it to go as deep in the wax as it did the previous time, by about a thirty-second of an inch, when it was cooled as before. In this way I dipt it from six to eight times, when I had a queen-cup that pleased me, as the outer edge was thinner than the bees made theirs, while the base was so thick that it would stand much more rough usage than would cells built by the bees. I now held it in the water, twirling it so that it would cool quickly, and, when cold, it was very easily taken off the stick or form, by twisting it a little. It could then be fastened to a comb, by dipping in melted wax, the same as I did with one of the cups.

I had now solved the mystery of queen-cell making, and, to make them quickly, I made more sticks, so that as soon as the wax had set on each, they could be laid on the table to cool, by placing them on a block [Fig. 5] having little notches in it.

In this way I could be dipping right along, while the wax on several sticks was cooling. I finally found that three were as many as I needed, for if the thin film first formed became too cold before it was dipt again, it did not work so well in taking the cells off.

Later on I dipt the stick deeper in the wax than at first, as I found that the bees would not reject so many of the cells when this was done. I find by measuring, that I now dip the sticks in the wax nine-sixteenths of an inch the first time (measuring from the extreme point), and dipping less and less each time, as before stated. so as to get the base of the cell very thick, which I consider a great advantage. A convenient way to get the right depth, is to raise one side of the lamp a little [Fig. 5, page 35], so that the wax will be deeper in one end of the dish, than at the other. Dip in the deep end first, having the wax deep enough in this end so that it will come to the right point on the stick when the end strikes the bottom, and keep going toward the shallow end, as you proceed.

By holding the stick, when lifted from the wax, at different angles while twirling it, the cell can be made heavy at any desired point. To keep the wax at the right depth, add a little occasionally, putting it in that part of the dish immediately over the lamp, so that it will melt quickly. To secure the best results, keep the wax just above the melting point, for, if too hot, it requires many more dippings to get the same thickness of cell, besides bothering in other ways.

The question now before me was, Would the bees accept these cups the same as they did the natural cups that I clipt off the combs ?   I feared not ; and in this I was right, as the first trial proved.   This was a disappointment to me, altho I had thought it might be so.

Fig. 5.—Some of the Paraphernalia used by a Queen-Breeder.

[EXPLANATION OF THE ABOVE ENGRAVING:—Beginning at the right hand side, we have 1st, a mailing-cage used in shipping queens; 2nd, the three forming-sticks, laid on the notcht-block while the wax is cooling; 3rd, the dish for cold water; 4th, the lamp having the dish of wax on top; 5th, a wire-cloth cage used in introducing queens; 6th, (near the front edge of the table) the ear-spoon used in scooping up the royal jelly; 7th, the stick used to place royal jelly in the queen-cup; 8th, a queen-cell protector, showing a hatcht cell in the same, with the stopper in place; 9th, (at the back side of the table) a stick having wax queen-cups at-tacht, showing their position on the stick.]

While studying over the matter, it came to me one night as I lay awake—why not put some royal jelly into these cups, the same as there was in the cells that I had always been suc-cessful with, when transferring larvæ in the swarming sea-son ? This seemed so reasonable that I could hardly wait for the middle of the day to come, when I could try it. At 10 o'clock the next day, I had a dozen cells prepared, each having some royal jelly in it ; then larvæ were placed in the royal jelly, the same as I always did when using the transposition process in swarming colonies. In this way the larvæ had an abundance of queen-food, even tho the workers did not feed them in from two or three hours to half a day, which was quite a step in advance of setting them in embryo queen-cups, with only the food that I could take up with the toothpick, as previously stated.

To get the royal jelly in the cups, I dipt a little of it out of a queen-cell that I took from a colony building cells, taking one that was nearly ready to seal, as such had the most jelly in it. After the large queen-larva was thrown out, the whole jelly was stirred up in the cell, so as to get all of one thickness, for that in the bottom of the cell will be found much thicker than that about the larva.

When thus mixt, the jelly was taken up with the ear-spoon on a pair of tweezers [Fig. 5, page 35], which was then transferred to the hollowed-out end of a little stick, by drawing the bowl of the ear-spoon over the end of the stick, until about one-eighth inch in diameter of the jelly was standing on the end of it. The end of the stick having the royal jelly on it, was then lowered into the bottom of the wax-cup, when it was twirled a little so as to make the jelly stay on the bottom of the cell, the same as it does when the bees place it there.

The amount of jelly used for each cup, was about the size of a " B B " shot, when on the end of the stick, before lowering into the cup, or one-eighth inch in diameter, as stated before. To get the first jelly of the season, a colony must be made queenless ; but after this, it is secured by taking one or two of the prepared cells at any time before they are sealed up.

Having the frame in readiness, it was given to a colony that was preparing to swarm, and left for two days. When I opened the hive this time, and drew out the prepared frame, you can imagine my pleasure at seeing twelve as nice queen-cells under headway as I ever saw, all looking like so many queen-cells built out of new comb—they were so light colored. In three days more these twelve cells were capt, and, in due time, twelve as splendid queens as I ever saw, hatcht from them. There was now no need of searching combs for embryo queen-cells, for I had something very much better, and something which would stand more rough usage than the other cups ever would endure.

My next idea was to have all of the queen-cells built on a stick, or piece of frame-stuff, the same as I had read about ; so when I again made some, instead of taking the cup off the form, I only loosened it enough so that it would slip off the stick easily, when it was again dipt in the wax and immediately placed on a mark on the piece of frame-stuff, which mark I had designated as a place for a cell [Fig. 6]. In an instant the cup had adhered to the frame-stuff, when the

Fig. 6.—Affixing the Wax-Cups to the Stick on which they are to be Built.

forming-stick was withdrawn. This cell was placed near the center of this stick, as to its length, but close to one side of it, as to width.

The next cell or cup was placed one and one-half inches to the right of the first, while the third was placed the same distance to the left, and so on until six were on the stick. I then put the next on the opposite side from the other six, and half way between them, so that when I had six more cups on, or twelve in all, the cells alternated with each other, which gave more room to each cell when occupying a given space, than would have been given, had I placed each along the center of the stick [Fig. 5, page 35.]

To get the designated places for cells, set the dividers the distance apart that you desire the cells, and after having put one of the points where you desire to have the first cell, "walk" them along until you make the number of point-marks that you want cells, and, in dipping, set a wax-cup over each point-mark.

Having the cells thus fixt, helpt in several ways, as it gave the bees a better chance to cluster among them in building, while it gave me a better chance to manipulate the cells in transferring the royal jelly and larvæ to them, taking them off, etc., and especially in getting them off the stick; for, when fixt in this way, all I had to do was to push gently on the outside of the base of the cell with my thumb, then off it came, without any danger of injuring it in anyway.

After dipping cells for some time, the forming-sticks will get so coated with wax that the water will stand in drops, instead of flowing freely over them, thus causing the cups to stick so as to spoil them in taking off. When this is the case, the stick is dipt in the water, and immediately placed between the second and third fingers of the left hand, close up to the hand, and twirled around once or twice, which causes the water to spread out over the stick; when it is dipt in the wax, and will work again as well as ever. When working continuously I am able to make from 150 to 200 cups in an hour, so it will be seen that but little time is required to make all that will be needed in any queen-rearing establishment.

I now had easy sailing all along the line, for all I had to do was to prepare the frame with these wax-cups, put in the royal jelly, which was now very easily done by laying the stick of cells bottom-side up on a table [Fig. 5, page 35] or chair before me, while the royal jelly was being disht into each; and before removing from the table, transfer the larvæ, taken from the hive having my best breeding queen, into each cell. When all was ready, this stick of prepared cells was crowded between the side-bars to a frame of comb, which had been previously cut so that the cells would come in the center of the comb, while the ends of the stick slipt through a slot cut in the comb for them. I keep several old combs, say ten or twelve for this purpose, which are used as often as cells are needed. This is a great convenience, and saves destroying or mutilating a valuable comb every time we want cells built.

By doing the whole in a warm room, I was independent of the weather, for in carrying the frame to the hive, I wrapt it in a warm flannel cloth, when it was at all cool outside. In this way I was sure to get a large proportion of the cells completed, whether used in a colony preparing to swarm, or in a colony which I had fixt for queen-rearing.

Before carrying to the hive, a slight shaving was taken from the top-bar of the frame, and the date placed on it, so I

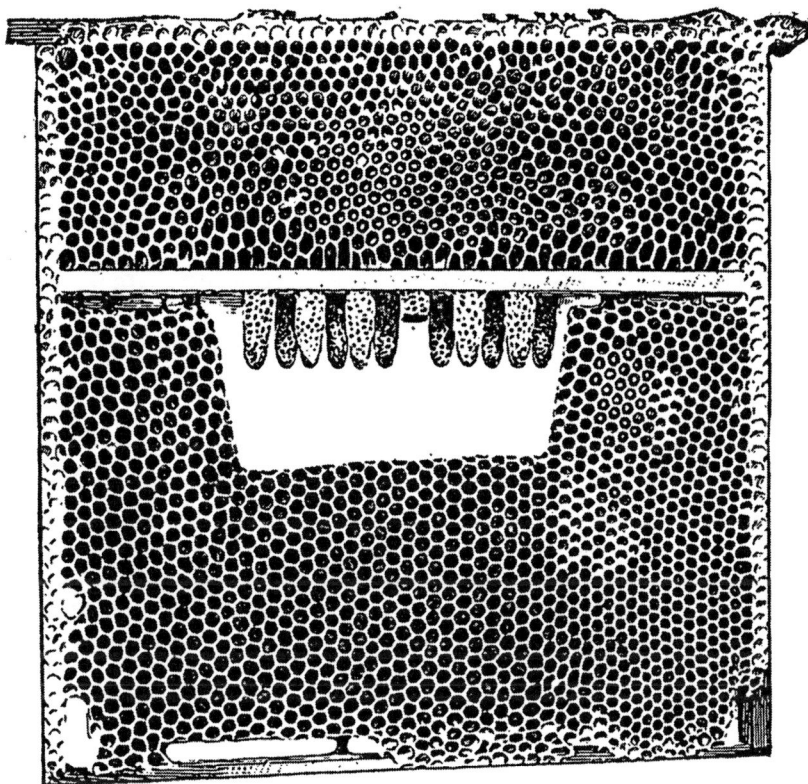

Fig. 7.—Frame with Stick of Queen-Cells.

EXPLANATION.—Frame showing how the stick of queen-cups is fitted into it, and how the cells look after being built from the cups. The illustration is less than one-fourth size, as the frame used is for the Gallup hive, which is 11¼x11¼ inches.

could know just when these cells would hatch. If the figures on it read "7-20," I knew that the cells were prepared July 20, and should be cared for on the 30th of that month. I then wrote in a small book kept for this purpose, "7-20 placed in hive No. 40" (if that happened to be the hive they were placed in), so that by looking at this book at any time, I knew where each frame of cells was, and when put there. If cells were started with larvæ from any but my best queen, the name of the queen was also placed on the frame and in the book, so that I knew just what I was about at all times. By looking in this book, I knew just when and where I should go to get these cells, so that none were destroyed by the queens hatching before I expected.

In getting larvæ for queen-rearing, when very cool, I placed the piece of brood under my clothing near my body, as soon as cut from the comb, and kept it there while carrying it to the room, so that there was no danger of chilling the larvæ ; or, if handier, as was sometimes the case, I placed it in a box having a heated iron in it, as will be explained farther along. A small room especially adapted for the handling of cells, brood, etc., which can be kept warm in cool weather, is almost a necessity to the man who makes a business of queen-rearing. When only a few queens are reared, the family kitchen can be used, as there is almost always a fire there—providing the "better half" is willing.

After working successfully along this line, with both swarming colonies and those made queenless for queen-rear-ing purposes, I chanced one day to find a colony which was about to supersede its queen, and gave evidence of being one of those colonies which might have two queens in a hive. I was not long in deciding to try my process of cell-building in this colony, so I at once destroyed the queen-cells which the bees had started, having royal jelly in them, using the royal jelly to put in the wax-cups I had prepared for them. I soon had the frame of prepared cells in the colony, when I waited rather impatiently for the next two days, till I could see what the developments would be.

At the end of two days, I went to the hive, and upon lift-ing out the frame I found that eleven out of the twelve cups prepared, had been accepted, and were now on the way to completion, as perfect queen-cells. Two days before the cells were ready to hatch, I had them photographt, and I have given the reader a fairly good picture of them [Fig. 7, page 39], which also represents these cells as built in an upper story over a queen-excluding honey-board, as about to be described.

To say that I was delighted with this success would hardly express it ; I was almost happy in thinking that I could now get queen-cells of the best type, and by the quantity, as long as I could keep that old queen alive at the head of the colony, for it was an exceedingly strong one.

Upon leaving this colony, I went to another strong one,

and removed its queen, so that I might have a place where I could put these cells' as soon as they were sealed, for safe keeping, till they were old enough to give to nuclei; for my object was to keep this colony rearing queens constantly, as long as the mother lived. As soon as the cells were sealed, they were removed and placed in the queenless colony, and another prepared frame given to them.

This last frame was accepted the same as the other, and, if my memory serves me rightly, this colony completed eleven sets of cells, before the old queen gave out entirely. At any rate, they reared so many that I saw the plan was a complete success, for all these queens were of the highest possible type, as to color, size and fertility; while the amount of royal jelly put in each cell was simply enormous, so much so that one cell taken from the frame would have jelly enough to start the twelve cups on a prepared frame at any time; while large quantities were left in the bottom of each cell, after the queens had hatcht out.

Before going farther, I must digress a little. In January, 1883, I met Mr. D. A. Jones, of Canada, at the "North-eastern" bee-convention, which was held that year at Syra-cuse, N. Y.; and in a private talk, regarding how to best secure the greatest yield of comb honey, he told me that he had found that he could get the most honey by having it built in the brood-chamber of the hive, fixing things so as to have the sections surrounded with brood, as it were.

To briefly describe the plan, as I now remember, it was as follows: When the honey season arrived, the brood-chamber was divided into three parts, the central one having five combs in it, which were to be enclosed with perforated-zinc, or, what we now term, queen-excluding division-boards. These five frames were to contain, as far as possible, only hatching brood, so that the queen might have room to lay, as the brood hatcht out. On either side of this small brood-chamber, sections were to be placed, by hanging in wide frames filled with them to the amount which it was thought that the colony required; while beyond these wide frames of sections, the remainder of the frames of brood, taken out when reducing the brood-chamber, were to be placed, having an equal number on each side.

In ten days the hive was to be opened, and the queen hunted, and, when found, the frame she was on was to be put outside, when the remaining four frames were put over to take the place of those outside of the sections, while those outside were to be placed in the brood chamber, and the frame having the queen on it returned. By treating the colony in this way every ten days, the queen furnisht as much brood as she otherwise would, while the sections were kept in the middle of the hive (so to speak), all of the while, which caused the bees to work assiduously to fill up this vacant space in the brood-nest, thus giving more honey than could be obtained in any other way.

This lookt so reasonable to me, that I accepted it at once ; but with the usual caution which I have always thought best

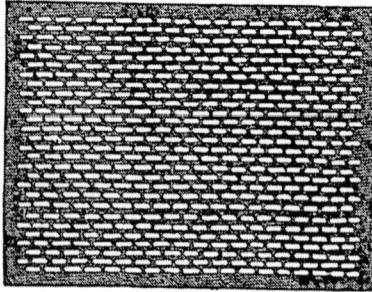

Fig. 8.—Queen-Excluding Division-Board.

to use, where trying something new, I made only two hives to be workt on this plan the following season. Without going into the details farther, suffice it to say that on account of pollen in the sections, and some other difficulties, the plan did not succeed with me as I had expected, so it was given up.

There was one thing that I learned, however, which started me on the road to a new discovery along the line of queen-rearing; which was, that in every case, where unsealed brood was placed outside of the sections, the bees would start from one to three queen-cells, and unless I cut them off, the queens hatching from them would supersede the old one, or else a swarm would be the result, when the combs having the cells on, were placed back with the queen again. This I did not like, as it was too much bother to look over the combs carefully, every ten days, in addition to the other work, when a change of combs was to be made.

One of the colonies so tried, had one of my best queens in it, and when I came to cutting off the cells, I was not slow to see that they might be made to form no small part in my queen-rearing business. However, the cutting of nice combs to get these cells stood in the way of my desiring to get all of my queens in that way, and besides, all the queens so reared did not please me, for the colony was often so spread out with sections between the brood, that the necessary heat to get good queens was not always present.

I now began using the queen-excluding metal [Fig. 8,

page 42], between the upper and lower stories of the few hives that I workt for extracted honey, and in one or two cases, brood from the lower story was placed in the upper one, over the queen-excluding honey-board. Again I had queen-cells built as in the former case, which were cared for as well as any I had ever seen, altho, as a rule, but two or three would be built on one lot of brood.

In thinking the matter over one night, while I was awake, doing some planning for the future, it came to me that these cells were built under precisely the same conditions that the cells were when the bees were thinking of superseding their queens, at which time I was enabled to get the best of queen-cells built. To be sure, the queen below was a good one, but as she could not get above, the brood that the bees had there did not increase any, so they concluded that they must have a better queen in this part of the hive; hence, they went to work to produce one.

One thing that I had always noticed was, that where the bees had their own way in the matter, where cells were built to supersede a queen while she was still in the hive, they never started more than three or four cells, while one or two were more often built than otherwise. That the bees only built about the same number in these cases of brood above a queen-excluding honey-board; and, also, that I have never known a swarm to issue, simply from having queen-cells in such an upper story, when none were below, shows that they consider the conditions the same as in case of supersedure.

Having become satisfied that I was right on this point, the next step was to see if the plan which had proved so success-ful with the colony about to supersede its queen, would work above the queen-excluding honey-board; and if it would, I would be a step farther in advance than I had ever been be-fore; for in it I saw something of great value to the bee-keeping fraternity in the future.

A frame of queen-cups was now prepared as before, and to make sure of success, if such a thing were possible, I raised two frames of brood (mostly in the larval form) above, so as to get as large a force of nurse-bees about the prepared cells as possible, to properly feed the queen-larvæ. The prepared frame was placed between the two having brood in them. In two days I examined this frame, and found that my conclu-sions were right, for every cup had grown to a half-built queen-cell, while the larvæ were floating in a quantity of royal jelly that more than half filled the cell. These were finisht in due time, and from them hatcht queens which were every whit as good as any I had ever seen.

I now had things brought to where I was master of the

situation, so that I could rear the best of queens, just when and just where I wanted them, and that, too, with a laying queen in the hive at all times, so there would be no loss in honey-production, to any apiarist, while rearing queens ; and the beauty of it all was, that these cells were all on a stick, so that they could be made use of without injuring any of my good combs, or in any way endangering any of the occupants of the cells.

Not knowing to what extent this plan could be carried, and yet secure good queens, I went slowly at first, not giving any one colony a second prepared frame till after the first had been removed and more brood placed above. As I leave the cells where they are built, till they are nearly ready to hatch, or for ten days, this took five colonies to give me a lot of queen-cells every other day, as I desired them, during the height of the season.

The next season, wanting to see how much there was in the plan, I put in a prepared frame as soon as the first cells were sealed, and then another as soon as these were sealed, and so on indefinitely. As far as I could see, the last lot of cells were as good as the first, altho, as a rule, I did not get quite as many accepted. It was a rare thing that the bees finisht less than nine out of twelve prepared cells during the first season, while the bees would frequently build and properly care for the whole twelve. In crowding them so fast, they would sometimes give me only five or six, yet, as a rule, they would average about eight, so that I really gained nothing by thus crowding things.

For this reason, I now kept along the line of work followed the first season, till the past summer, when, to see what might be accomplisht, preparatory to writing this book, I gave a prepared frame to a colony every two days, and, while they did not complete as many cells on each frame as formerly, when I gave them less often, yet some cells would be built on every frame.

In this way I had in one colony having a laying queen below, queen-cells in all stages of progress, from those just ready to hatch, down to larvæ that the bees had just commenced to feed, by adding to the royal jelly which I had placed in the cups ; and besides this, I had queens kept in nurseries in different parts of the upper story. I also had in the same upper story, queens just hatcht, and some just commencing to lay, by having a part of the upper hive formed into nuclei, by using perforated-metal division-boards, as will be explained farther on. It will be seen that there is scarcely any limit to what can be accomplisht by this method of queen-rearing, and queen-fertilizing.

However, as a rule, I think that a little better queens can be reared by the way I workt the plan the first season, for the cells are better supplied with queen-food, where unsealed brood is placed in the upper story every ten days—enough better, in my opinion, to pay for the extra work.

Again, I would not put over twelve wax-cups on a stick, for if more are used the young queens are not fed quite as well. In my experiments I have used as high as twenty-four cups, and had every one accepted and finisht; but unless the colony was an extremely populous one, I did not get quite as good queens as when only twelve were used.

To show what may be accomplisht by this method, I will say, that in the honey harvest I have prepared sticks having from four to eight cups on them, the sticks being made of the right length to crowd into any section of the hive that I was using, so as to keep it from falling down, when the section was placed between two others, in which the bees were at work over a queen-excluding honey-board; when upon going to the hive at the end of ten days, I would find as nice queen-cells, nearly ready to hatch, as any one needs to see.

I have also had queens fertilized and kept till they were laying, one in each section of the hive, yet this plan of producing queens in sections is not to be recommended, as it spoils the section from being first-class for honey, ever afterward.

By way of caution, I wish to say, that if a queen is by any means allowed to hatch in the same apartment where the cells are, these cells will at once be destroyed. If the bees with such a queen are shaken off the combs, so as to get her out of the way of more cells being built, and the bees are allowed to enter the hive below, with this queen (as would be natural for any apiarist to do), this young queen will destroy the one below, no matter how prolific or how valuable a queen you may have there. This queer procedure I bring to bear on all queens that I wish to supersede, as will be explained farther on.

Another thing: In the fall (or in this locality after Aug. 15), when the bees begin to be inactive, or cease brood-rearing to any great extent, the warmth generated in the upper story will not be enough to produce good queens, and as the season draws toward a close, no queen-cells will be completed, unless we feed sufficiently to arouse the whole colony into activity, and keep them thus all the time while the cells are being built. At such times I have had cells that usually mature in eleven and one-half days, to be from sixteen to twenty days before hatching; while the queens would be almost black, from the same brood which produced very yellow queens during June, July, and the first half of August.

In all parts of the country where fall flowers abound, I presume just as good queens will be reared in September by this plan, as at any time; but as we have no fall flowers here, I cannot be positive on this point.

At any time when the bees work the cells very slowly, I know no better plan than that which was given in the last chapter, only I use the wax cells, prepared with royal jelly, as given before. Then in early spring, before the colonies are strong enough to go into the upper stories, we must use that way also, for there are not enough bees in any hive to use the above method, which I believe to be the best of all. However, much can be done by way of getting a colony strong, by giving sealed brood, so this last process can be used much earlier in the season than otherwise would be the case.

In this chapter, I think that I have given something of great value to the fraternity; and if it shall lead to the universal rearing of a better class of queens than have formerly been reared, I shall be well paid for all my efforts in this direction.

CHAPTER VIII.

GETTING THE BEES OFF THE CELLS.

It would hardly seem that a chapter should be devoted to this subject, but from what I know of others doing along this line, and what I used to do myself, I am satisfied that many queens are materially injured before they are out of the cells, and many more are killed outright. We frequently see in print, the instruction given, when handling frames after the bees have swarmed and before the queen-cells have hatcht, that to get the bees off the combs the "frames should be shaken," or "the bees shaken off in the usual way." Many write asking why their queen-cells do not hatch, or why so many queens hatch with crippled wings, or having a dent in one side of the abdomen. When answering such an inquiry, and asking for more particulars, these almost always reveal that they have shaken the frame having the cells on, to get the bees off.

One man came a long distance for some brood from my best queen, from which to rear some queens to cross with his stock; and after securing some 50 or 60 splendid cells from this brood, by the transposition process, he came after more brood, telling me that out of the whole lot, only three queens hatcht, and only one of those being perfect. Upon asking him how he got the bees off the frames having the queen-cells on them, he said he shook them off, the same as he always did. It does not seem that any one would be so thoughtless, yet there are hundreds who do not stop to think of these little things.

I wish to emphasize the words, *never shake the bees off a frame having queen-cells on it, nor in any way suddenly jar it !* for queen-cells are much more liable to injury while on the frame, than they are when taken from where they were built. The reason for this lies in the fact that when the comb is moved, there is a heavier body than in a single cell; hence, the heavy body takes more force to move it than does the lighter one, which is apt to give it an accelerated speed, and when suddenly brought to a stop, it causes a concussion much greater than the operator dreams of; while this concussion sets the queen pupa to tumbling around in its cell, to a very damaging extent, and one nearly, if not quite as great, as would come to it had the tree in its forest home, as provided by Nature, been suddenly blown over by some thunder-gust. Under such circumstances, no one would expect queen-cells to hatch. Care should always be used in handling cells, but especially before they are removed from the combs or frames. My way of doing this is as follows;

Having lifted the frame with the cells on it, from the hive, it is carefully put down near the entrance, letting it rest on the bottom-bar, so that it will occupy the same position that it did in the hive. To thus fix it without killing the bees which may be on the under side of the bottom-bar, I lower it so that it will touch the short grass which grows about the sides of the hive, and then, by drawing the frame endwise toward the entrance, the bees are all brusht off on the grass, so that none are left where they would be killed. This is the way I always do, when putting the frame on the ground for any purpose.

Having the frame near the entrance, and leaning up against the hive, I smoke the bees thoroughly, so as to cause them to fill themselves with honey, and while they are doing this, I arrange the interior of the hive, when it is closed. I then smoke the bees some more, and if they seem inclined to leave the comb and run into the hive, I keep smoking them until all have run in; but if they are loth to leave the comb, which they usually are, I take hold of the frame and raise it a foot or so above the entrance, when, with one of the soft bee-brushes now used by most bee-keepers, or with the feather end of a quill from a turkey's wing, the bees are brusht off, brushing about the cells very carefully.

If the bees have filled themselves with honey, they are rolled off the comb with the brush very easily, and seldom offer to sting; but if you undertake to brush them, when the frame is first lifted from the hive, you will find that they will stick to the comb and cells "like tigers," while their fury will be scarcely less than would be shown by the tiger herself, if pusht around while being robbed of her cubs.

Where frames of queen-cells are obliged to be handled on a cool day, or in a rain-storm, it is sometimes best to take them, bees and all, into the warmed room where the work is done with cells. When there, remove the cells as quickly as possible, allowing the bees to remain on the comb, which they will generally do if we do n'ot smoke them very much while removing the frame from the hive. Upon reaching the room, they will begin to fill themselves, and if spry, we can remove the cells while they are filling, and carry them back to the hive without losing any.

Once having the cells in the warm room, we need be in no hurry, for if the room is of the right temperature (from 85° to 95°), the inmates of the cells are advancing toward maturity just as fast as they would be in the hive.

CHAPTER IX.

WHAT TO DO WITH THE QUEEN-CELLS.

Having the queen-cells all built, and being nearly ready to hatch, with the bees all off from them, the next thing we want to know, is what to do with them.

There are three ways generally employed in using them, the one used most being to give the cells to nuclei or queen-less colonies; next, putting the frame having the cells on, in a lamp-nursery, leaving them there, and taking out the queens as fast as they hatch; and, lastly, putting each cell in a separate cage having food in it; while the cages are so arranged that from twelve to twenty-four of them will just go inside of a frame, filling it solid the same as a comb would; when the frame of cages is placed in the center of a full colony of bees, where it is left till the queens hatch, when they are to be disposed of as thought best.

The last is called a queen-nursery, and has the advantage over the lamp-nursery, in the fact that no watching is required to keep the queens from killing one another, should several hatch during the night, or when the apiarist was at other duties. As I wish to say something about each method, I will speak of them in the order named above.

As a chapter will soon be given on forming nuclei, all that I shall say in this will be in regard to how it is best to get the cells into these nuclei, or into a full colony, if you wish to put them there. Bear in mind, that if you wish to be sure that the cells are not torn down, you must wait about giving them to any colony, whether weak or strong, from 24 to 48 hours after their laying queen has been taken away; or, in other words, the colony must be queenless for that many hours before it is time to take the cells from the colony where they were built.

Some claim that an unprotected queen-cell can be given to a colony at the time a laying queen is taken from the same; but all of my experience goes to prove that where this is done, nine out of every ten cells thus given will be destroyed. I am not alone in this, for many prominent apiarists write me that they can do no better. However, I will say that it may be that I do not have my colonies small enough, for a colony so small that there is not over 200 bees in it will accept of a queen or a queen-cell much more readily than will a colony of 20,000 workers.

In giving queen-cells to colonies, if the weather is warm enough so that there is no danger of chilling the cells, or say when the mercury is at 75° or above, I take the frame of cells in my hand, and go to the nuclei with it (unless there is danger of robbing, from scarcity of honey in the fields), and put the frame of cells down next to the hive containing the nucleus or colony, the same as it was placed at the entrance of the hive in getting the bees off, so as to be sure that the cells are not injured in any way.

I then open the hive, and, having selected the spot on the comb where I wish to put the cell, I place my thumb on the base of one of the queen-cells and gently bear down, when it cleaves off the bar of wood to which it was fastened, as easily as need be. Now, instead of cutting the combs and fitting the cells into them, the way we always used to do, all I have to do is to place the cell against the side of the comb where I wish it to stay, and gently push against the base of the cell, when it sinks into the comb far enough to make it a fixture. After this comb is lowered into the hive, and the next comb brought up to it, this next comb touches the cell on the opposite side, so that it cannot fall out, even if the bees do not stick it fast, which they are almost sure to do, even if the other comb does not touch it.

Here is another advantage that these cells have over those entirely made by the bees, in that the wax is so thick at the base of the cell that it is impossible to dent them with any reasonable handling; also, this mode of putting on the comb keeps the nice worker-combs from being injured, as was the case with the old process, given in nearly all of our bee-literature.

If robber-bees are so that they will follow around, trying to get at the frame of honey with the queen-cells, the same is taken to the shop, or other room where I work, when the cells are taken off the bar of wood, in the same way as described before, and placed in a little basket that I have for the purpose, as fast as they are removed.

Why I use a basket in preference to anything else is because in warm weather this lets the air around the cells, it being of open-work, so that when the sun strikes on them there is not nearly the danger of over-heating that there otherwise would be. In a tin dish, when left in the sun, it takes only a moment or two to spoil the inmates of the cells by over-heating, while on hot days I have to be careful, even with the basket. Upon going to the apiary, the cells are now taken from the basket and used as before.

If the weather is very warm, or the colony to which the cell is given, is a strong one, I do not take out a frame when inserting the cell, but simply spread the top-bars apart a little, and crowd the cell lightly between them so that it will stay. This works equally well, if we are sure that the colony is strong enough to cluster around it, so as to keep it warm; but in all cool weather the other is the safest plan; as in the first case, I always put the base of the cell just above the brood, so that the point comes down on the brood, which insures the bees caring for it, as surely as they care for the brood.

If the weather is cooler than 75° in the shade. I heat one of the largest weights to my scales (any iron will do) so warm that I can just hold it in my hands, when it is dropt into a wooden box of sufficient size to let it slip into it, and over the weight is placed several thicknesses of felt, cut to fit the box. The cells are now placed on the felt, when a cover for the cells, made by sewing two or three pieces of the same felt together, and having a little handle attacht, is placed over them. The cells are now protected from the cold, so that I can go right on with my work regardless of the weather.

When I go to a hive, all I have to do is to lift the felt

cover by the handle, take out the cell and put back the cover. If you have more cells than you think the iron will keep up the necessary heat for, all you have to do is to leave the rest in the warm room until you can return and heat the iron again.

An oil-stove is very handy to keep this room warm, or to heat the iron or anything else with, and has the advantage in allowing you to control the temperature of the room perfectly, by turning the wicks up or down. However, any stove, or any room having one window in it, will answer all purposes, for any one who has not things fitted for this special work.

What I have to say about the lamp-nursery will be brief; for, to tell it just as it is, I have very little use for it, and none whatever in the way it is generally used. I do not like to be obliged to watch as closely as is necessary to keep the queens from killing one another while hatching; besides, the gain when used in this way is very little if any, where the cells can be left in the colony building them, until they are nearly ready to hatch, as is the case with the plan of cell-building which has been given. By the old ways, where the colony was kept nearly, or quite idle, from the time the cells were sealed till they were ready to hatch, the time saved to the colony by taking them to the lamp-nursery as soon as sealed, undoubtedly paid; but where the work of the colony is going on just the same, whether there are cells in the hive or not, the case is different.

The only time when I use it, is early in the spring or late in the fall, when I have to get the cells built in queenless colonies, and then I use it only in connection with the queen-nursery, which does away with all watching, or sitting up at night to see to the queens.

Were it not for the traffic in virgin queens, which is now growing, and bids fair to assume gigantic proportions, and the few times when we have more queen-cells ready to mature than we have just at that time small colonies to take them, there would be little more use for the queen-nursery than for the lamp-nursery.

For these reasons, however, I think that the use of the queen-nursery pays well; for it allows us to sort the virgin queens in sending them off, so we need send only the best; while it many times enables us to save a nice lot of queens which we would otherwise lose.

In using it, I put it in the upper story of any colony having a queen-excluder between it and the lower story; often putting it in the same apartment where the bees are rearing queens, as it makes no difference to the bees as regards cell-building, the work going on just the same if there are fifty virgin queens caged in the same apartment. At first I feared that cell-building would stop, or the cells already built would be destroyed, but after testing the matter I find that queens thus caged have no influence along these lines whatever.

The kind of nursery that I prefer, is like the one [Fig. 9] invented by Mr. Alley, and described in his book; but if my memory serves me rightly, Dr. Jewell Davis was the first one to bring the queen-nursery before the public.

I make the queen-nursery as follows: Sixteen blocks are gotten out, $2\frac{5}{8}$x$2\frac{5}{8}$x$\frac{7}{8}$ of an inch, which exactly fill one of my frames. A one-and-one-half inch hole is bored in the

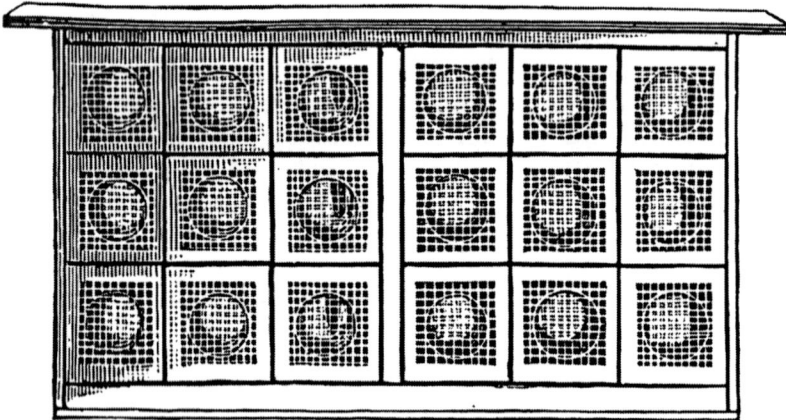

Fig. 9.—Queen-Nursery.

centre of each of these blocks, over which is tackt a piece of wire-cloth having twelve to sixteen meshes to the inch, and being two inches square.

Before tacking on the wire-cloth, I bore in the edge of the block (which is designated for the top after the block is put in the frame) a three-fourths inch hole, boring down to within one-eighth of an inch of the one-and-one-half inch hole. I now finish boring the hole with a one-half inch bit. This hole is for the queen-cell to be placed in, and the reason for the two sizes of holes is to give a shoulder, so that the queen-cell can hang in the block the same as it does on the comb and still be in no danger of slipping through into the block. This hole is bored a little to one side of the centre, so as to allow room for a one-half inch hole on the other side, which is to receive the candy; the latter hole is so bored that it comes out near one side of the one-and-one-half inch hole, and when it is deep enough, so that a hole large enough for the queen to enter is made, I stop boring, for a shoulder at the bottom is needed to keep the candy in place [Fig. 10]. Now fill the hole with candy, packing it in with a plunger made to fit the hole loosely, and tack on the wire-cloth. The blocks can be made so that a given number will fit any frame in use. I only gave this description as the right size to use in the Gallup frame.

Having the cages provisioned with the "Good" candy, made of granulated sugar and honey (granulated sugar is preferable to the powdered, to use in these cages), the cells are taken off the frames as before, when a little honey is put around the end, just where the queen will bite off the cover in hatching, so that she can feed herself before com-

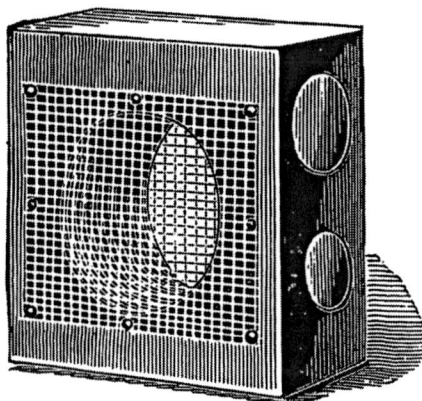

Fig. 10.—Nursery-Cage.

ing out of the cell, the same as the bees feed her when she hatches in the hive. When first using the nursery I did not know of this "trick," consequently I lost many queens by their not having strength to get out of their cells; but when I saw the bees feeding a queen one day, through an opening in the cell, I took the hint, and have had no trouble since.

After the cell has the honey on it (do not put on enough so that it will daub the queen), the cell is put in the hole made for it, and the cage put in the nursery-frame, and so on till all are in, when the nursery is taken to the hive and put where it will be kept warm by the bees.

If in the early spring or late in the fall it is put in the lamp-nursery, which is then kept running, as the heat in the hive is not great enough at this season of the year to hatch queens where the cells are in a nursery. I have lost many queens, even after they had hatcht, when trying to keep them in the nursery, placed in a colony after the bees had become partially inactive in the fall; so the queen-nursery is of no value in this locality after Sept. 15, unless it is used in connection with a lamp-nursery. If all has been done as it should be, there will be a splendid queen in each cage, in due time, ready to use when wanted.

In all of this work with cells they should, as far as possible, be kept in the same position as they are in the hive, and if laid down it should be done very gently so as not to injure the young queen within.

Before putting in another lot of cells in the cages, place a drop of honey on top of the food in the candy-hole, instead of renewing the candy; for this honey will work its way down through the sugar, so as to be where the queen can get it when she hatches, which is as good as to renew the candy each time.

CHAPTER X.

THE QUEEN-CELL PROTECTORS.

Some few years ago, after becoming disgusted by losing many queen-cells in trying to get the bees of a colony to accept such, as soon as a laying queen had been taken away (as some claim can be done), I resolved that I never would again lose a nice lot of queen-cells, by trying to save from 24 to 48 hours time to my nuclei, as I had so often done in trying what proved to be (with me) an impossibility. In so deciding, I felt somewhat sad, for "time," with the queen-breeder, "is money," in the summer months. However the loss of queen-cells was of more money value than the loss of time to the nuclei, hence I was driven to the above decision, altho with great reluctance.

That afternoon Mrs. Doolittle was away from home, not expecting to be back till in the evening; so when it grew so dark that I could see to work no longer, I went into the house, and, being rather dissatisfied with myself, in having to own up as being entirely beaten by the bees, on account of the above, I threw myself on the couch, instead of reading or answering correspondents, as is my custom generally before retiring. Being fatigued, I soon fell asleep, and slept about an hour.

Upon waking, the first thought that came to me was, why not make a cage of wire-cloth to protect the queen-cell, so that the bees could not get at the side of the cell until they became aware that they were queenless, which would be at about the time the cell would hatch; and in this way be victor, instead of owning up beaten, as I did a little while ago? Very soon the picture of a cage and all how to use it, stood out before me so plainly that I could see it with my mind as distinctly as I ever saw any picture with my eyes.

The idea of caging queen-cells was old, and cages especially adapted to this purpose had been advertised for a good many years; but the ideal cage presented before me at this time, was for the special purpose of allowing the safe introduction of a queen-cell, nearly mature, to a colony at the time of taking away a laying queen, the cage being so constructed that the queen could hatch and walk right out among the bees, the same as if no cage was there; while at the same time the cell was safely secured against the bees, so that they would not destroy it.

All are aware that when bees destroy a cell, they bite into the side or base of it, and never at the point, on account of the cocoon being so thick at the point end that they cannot make much headway in trying to get a hole in there. Well, the cage I saw on awaking, was to be made so as to protect all parts of the cell from the bees except the point, and this was not easy for them to get at, even if they did try to bite through it at this place.

The cage was made by rolling a small piece of wire-cloth around a V-shaped stick, so that a small but not very flaring funnel was made, the hole in the small end being as large as an ordinary lead-pencil. After making the cage, I cut off a piece of five-eighths inch cork for a stopper, put in a nearly mature queen-cell, with the point down into the lead-pencil hole as far as it would go, when the piece of cork was put in so that the bees could not get in at the base. [Fig. 5, page 35.]

I now took a fine wire and run it through the meshes of the wire-cloth just above the cork, so as to keep the cork in place, while the other end of the wire was bent so that it would hold on to the top of the frames, in order to keep the cage in the position I desired it, between the combs. These caged cells were hung in the hives at the time the queens were removed, and in from 24 to 48 hours, according to the age of the cell, I had a nice virgin queen in the hive wherever a caged cell was hung.

As soon as I found it was a success, I made many more cages, so that now I have no more trouble with bees destroying cells, not having over two percent destroyed out of the thousands so caged during the past three years. The cage protects the cell everywhere except at the point, but allows the bees to get accustomed to the presence of it, the same as if the cage was not there. The lead-pencil hole allows the queen to hatch the same as if the cell were not caged, while the bees can feed the queen and hold her in the cell as long as they please. The few cases where queens are killed seem to come about by the bees destroying them after they have been let out of the cell; yet I have thought that in a very few instances the bees had torn away the extreme end of the cell and dragged the queen out; but the instances of queens being destroyed where cells are so caged are so few that the plan can justly be called a success.

Instead of using cork for stoppers, I now use a piece of corn-cob, which will fit nicely in the cage, above the base of the cell; and instead of hanging the cage in the hive with a wire, I press the cage into the comb, the same as I have told of doing with an uncaged cell. In pressing the cage into the comb, bear on the cob, for in this way there is no danger of pressing the meshes of the wire-cloth into the cell; and only press it far enough so that the cage is secure to the comb. In this way the bees will not gnaw through the septum to the comb, so as to injure it, if the cage is left in the hive for several days after the queen hatches, as they are sure to do if the cage is prest down till it strikes the center of the comb.

When I have many queens to send off, in days when there is danger of over-heating the cells, or chilling them, I put up the queens first, then take the caged cells in the basket or heated box and put them in afterward, the same as is done with uncaged cells.

Some who have tried this plan of caging cells, have complained that they had to trim the cell so much to get it into the cage, that it made lots of work, which is the truth, where the old plans of cell-building are used; but with the plan of wax-cells, as here given, all of this trimming part is done away with. This also accounts for the reason that some have not succeeded with them, for the cells built by the old plans would not fit the cages so well but that the bees could get at them to bite in at the sides of the cell.

This caging of cells is of great value, where queens are

placed in the upper story of full colonies, for fertilization, as is soon to be described; for in this case I have never had one destroyed, even when put in but a few hours previous to their hatching.

CHAPTER XI.

HOW TO FORM NUCLEI.

There are nearly as many ways of forming nuclei as there are different individuals who make them; yet that does not alter the old saying that, "there is a right and a wrong way" to do almost anything. Many of the plans employed are very poor, to say the least, as I have proven by trying nearly all of the methods given. Of these poor methods I will not speak, for there are plenty of plans which are fairly good, hence I can see no reason for any one using a poor method.

The plan in most general use, is to go to any colony which can spare the bees—between the hours of 10 a. m. and 2 p. m., when the bees are flying briskly, so that most of the old bees are from home—and take a frame of brood and one of honey, together with all of the adhering bees, being careful not to get the old queen, and put the frames into a hive where you wish the nucleus to stand. The bees are now to be confined to the hive for 48 hours, so that they will not go back to their former location, and, just at night, they are to be set at liberty, and a queen-cell given them, when in a week or so they will have a laying queen.

The frame of brood should have plenty of young bees just hatching from the cells, and to make sure that you do not have the old queen, she should be found, and the frame which she is on put outside of the hive while you take the other two frames out. This plan does very well where there are but few nuclei to be made, and has the advantage of being so simple that even those most unaccustomed to bee-keeping can understand it.

A plan fully as simple, and one which I like better (inasmuch as the bees need no confining), is to make a colony queenless, thus causing it to rear queens, as given in Chapter VI, only using the wax-cells with royal jelly in them. As soon as the cells are sealed over, give the colony all of

the frames of hatching brood that they can care for, so as
to make it a powerful colony; when, two days before the
queens should hatch, a cell is to be transferred to each of
the combs, by pushing the base of the cell into the comb,
as I have explained.

On the next day, each frame having a cell on it, is to be
carried to a hive where you want a nucleus to be, and after
placing it inside the same, a frame of honey is to be given
drawing up the division-board so as to adjust the hive to
the size of the colony. Now from any hive take a frame of
brood, and after shaking the bees off from it, carry it to the
now combless hive whose colony reared the queen-cells,
fasten a cell to it (which should have been reserved for this
purpose), and leave the frame in this hive to be taken care
of by the bees that were not taken with the removed combs,
and those which will return from the fields. In this way,
from five to ten nuclei can be made from one colony, according to the time of year when the plan is practiced.

Both of these plans are to be employed only where cells
are given, for the first will not receive a virgin queen, and
the last will not stay with a strange virgin queen as well as
they will with one of their own cells.

However, it often happens that we have more young
queens than we have nuclei to care for them, and as we
wish to save these, and also get along just as fast as possible, I experimented until I found a plan whereby young
queens from one to five days old could be introduced, and
nuclei formed at the same time, so that the day after the
bees were liberated they would have a fertilized queen.

The way of doing this, is to make a wire-cloth frame
that will fit into a hive, and yet admit one of the frames
from the hive inside of it, which should also have a cover
fitted over the top, so that no bee can get out. Now take a
frame having much brood about to hatch, and hang it in
the wire-cloth cage, when one of the young queens that you
have on hand is to be allowed to run down inside the cage.
Next, put on the cover, and hang the cage in any hive where
the colony is strong enough to keep up the desired temperature. If you have an upper story on any hive, this is the
best place to put it, for it requires more room for the cage
and frame than it does for the frame without the cage, as
there must be from one-fourth to three-eighths of an inch
between the wire-cloth and the comb. If you use a lamp-
nursery, and can control the temperature perfectly, this
caged frame may advantageously be put in that.

In four or five days from the time the frame was put in
the cage, take the cage from the hive (when you will find

it pretty well filled with bees, providing that you made a good choice in the selection of the frame of hatching brood), and carry it to the hive where you wish it to remain. Now put the cage down near the entrance of the hive, take off the cover, and after having removed the frame from the cage, put it in the hive, placing a frame of honey beside it; adjust the division-board, and after closing the hive, shake the bees out of the cage near the entrance, when some of them will run in, with the call of "Home is found."

In making this change, probably many bees will fly in the air; but if the cage was left at the entrance, as it should be, all will enter the hive when through their play-spell.

In one or two cases the queen was fertilized on the day they were put in the hive, but usually not until the next day.

This plan has the advantage over the others, inasmuch as there is no danger of any bees leaving the nucleus; and also, that about as soon as formed they have a laying queen. After having all in readiness, nuclei can be made in this way with very little trouble, and I like the method very much.

There is also another way of making a nucleus, and introducing a virgin queen of any age, which I use more often at the present time than any other; and as a part of the process applies to the safe introduction of queens received through the mails when we do not expect them, I will give the plan at length.

First, make what I have termed a "nucleus-box," as follows: Take two pieces of wood, six inches long by six wide, and three-fourths of an inch thick; to them nail two pieces twelve inches long by six wide, and one-fourth of an inch thick, so as to make a box ten-and-one-half inches long by six wide, and six inches deep, inside measure, without sides.

I next take two pieces of wire-cloth, twelve inches long by six-and-one-half inches wide, one of which is permanently nailed to one side of the box, while the other is nailed to four strips which are one-fourth of an inch square, these strips going round the outer edge of the wire-cloth. Through the center of these strips is driven a five-eighths inch wire-nail, so as to fasten this wire-cloth to the opposite side of the box in such a way as to make it readily removable at any time, with an ordinary pocket-knife. In the centre of the top of the box, bore a hole of the right size to admit the small end of a funnel, to be made of tin, and large enough so that you can shake the bees off the frames into it, the same as is done in putting up bees by the pound. Over this hole fix a slide, button, or something of the kind, so that the hole can be closed quickly, when you wish to do so, when taking out the funnel or putting in a queen.

Having the box and funnel made, go to any hive having an upper story with a queen-excluder under it (so that there will be no danger of getting the old queen), and take out two combs well covered with bees, if you want a good-sized nucleus ; or only one comb if you desire a small nucleus Put these combs on the ground, resting them against the hive, then jar them a little, by rapping on the comb with a stick, knife-handle, or the thumb-nail, so as to cause the bees to fill themselves with honey. As soon as the bees are filled, shake them off the combs into the funnel, and they will roll down through the hole into the box.

Take the funnel out of the box, and close the hole, when, after putting the combs in the hive and closing it, take the box to the bee-cellar, or any dark, cool place, and leave it.

If more than one nucleus is to be made, I go to other hives, and take out frames, the same as I did at first, thus keeping at work while the bees are filling themselves with honey; in this way as many nuclei can be made as we have boxes, doing the work of getting them into the boxes as soon as the bees are filled with honey.

To secure the best results, and have the small colonies so that they can be cared for at about sunset, they should be made between the hours of 9 and 11 a. m. If it is not handy to carry the boxes of bees to a room or cellar, I simply put them on the shady side of the hive, and place an empty hive or hive-cover over them, leaving them where they are.

In less than an hour these bees will almost "cry" for a queen of some kind; but as they will sometimes cluster (or ball) a queen if given too soon, especially where virgin queens are used, I wait from 3 to 4 hours, when they will fairly "beg" for a queen. I now get as many virgin queens, from 4 to 8 days old, as I have boxes of bees, and put them in with the bees. All I do in putting them in, is to set the box down suddenly, thus jarring the bees all to the bottom, so that they will be out of the way while I have the hole open, then put the queen down through the hole.

The box is now left until nearly sunset, when the bees will be found all quiet, and clustered like a swarm. To have it so that the movable side of wire-cloth can be taken off without disturbing the cluster, I incline the box when leaving it, after putting the queen in, so that the bees will cluster away from this side.

They are now hived in a hive, having in it a frame of

honey, and a frame having some sealed or hatching brood in it. If possible, do not give them any unsealed brood, for, if you do, they will sometimes kill the queen, and rear cells from the brood given. It is not natural for a colony to have an oldish virgin queen at the same time they have eggs and larvæ; for in Nature, all brood would be sealed before the young queens were three days old.

To hive them, I put the frame of brood and honey on one side of the hive, together with the division-board, when, with a quick jar, I dislodge all of the bees from the box, on the bottom of the hive, near the opposite side. I now quickly slide the combs and the division-board across the rabbets to this side of the hive, when the bees are immediately on them. In three or four days more, this young queen is fertilized and laying, when the nucleus is ready for sending off queens at once, with less time and labor than it takes to get a laying queen in any other way.

All nuclei, in whatever manner made, should be put close to one side of the hive, having a division-board drawn up to the combs which the bees occupy; while the entrance should be on the opposite end of the hive, at the bottom, else the nuclei may suffer from being robbed by strong colonies in times of honey-dearth. Since I began thus to arrange my nuclei in hives, I have not had one robbed; while previous to this I was much annoyed from this source.

In these four methods, I have given the reader the "cream" of all the plans now in use, without their having to go over scores of methods of making nuclei, as I was obliged to do. At all times when bees are working in upper stories, I consider the last plan the best yet known.

CHAPTER XII.

HOW TO MULTIPLY NUCLEI.

After each queen has commenced to lay, she should be allowed to stay in the hive a day or two before sending her off, so as to supply the combs with eggs, thus keeping up the strength of the nucleus. If she does as well as she ought to, and if we get a laying queen as often as we should, one-half or more of the nuclei will begin to get stronger than they need to be, to secure the best results; for it is generally known that queens will commence to lay sooner, and be received much quicker, in rather weak nuclei, than they will in those which are very strong.

For this reason, and also not wanting to take any more bees from my full colonies than I could possibly avoid, I have been in the habit of "multiplying nuclei," as I term it, every time that I came across a strong nucleus where there were many young bees hatching from the combs; and doing this as long as I want an increase of such small colonies.

As already stated in a former chapter, bees will adhere to combs on which is a nearly-mature queen-cell, when carried to a new location, much more closely than they will adhere to frames of brood; but nothing will hold bees to a new location equal to a queen that has just commenced to lay.

Taking advantage of this fact, I place an extra comb in all nuclei which I think will be strong enough to spare one from it, by the time the queen commences to lay. After she begins to lay, she is left till there are eggs in the two combs, when the comb having the most mature brood in it (together with the queen and all adhering bees) is taken to a new hive, thus starting up a new colony. The two combs left in the old hive are now brought together, a caged queen-cell given to the remaining bees, and the hive closed. A frame of honey is given to the bees and queen in the new hive, the division-board adjusted, and that hive is also closed. They are now left in this way for three days, when the queen is sent off, and the bees are given a caged cell.

Where queens are reared in large quantities for market, this plan of multiplying nuclei is of great advantage, and I have used it very largely during previous years. A little practice will enable any one to know when these small colonies are strong enough to be divided, and convince him that this is the quickest and simplest way of making nuclei now known.

When through with these nuclei in the fall, enough of them are put together, or united, to form a good colony for wintering. To do this I send off queens enough on one day, or otherwise dispose of them, so that the number of nuclei un-queened will make a good colony. I now proceed to cause the bees in each to fill themselves with honey, when they are shaken down through the funnel into the box used in forming nuclei, and treated in the same way, by giving them a queen, hiving them, etc.

I am glad, however, to tell the reader that all this work of forming nuclei and uniting them will soon be a thing of the past; for in the next chapter you will find a more excellent way of getting queens fertilized than by the use of nuclei. The near future will see all virgin queens fertilized in full colonies, each colony having a laying queen.

CHAPTER XIII.

QUEENS FERTILIZED IN THE SAME HIVE WHERE THERE IS A LAYING QUEEN.

To secure the fertilization of queens, without having to form nuclei, has been a hobby of mine for years. By this I do not mean what is called "fertilization in confinement," as my faith in this has always been small, altho I have spent much time in this direction; and right here I wish to say, that I cannot help thinking that in all cases of success reported there must have been a mistake somewhere; else why could not such men as Prof. A. J. Cook, L. C. Root, and hosts of other practical bee-men, who have tried all of the plans ever given to the public, have had just one case of success? As nearly as I am able to learn, all who have reported success were either novices in the business or were those who conducted their experiments so loosely that there was a chance that their queens became fertilized by the ordinary way, at some time when the experimenter might have been found "napping."

My hobby has been that of letting the queens fly out to meet the drones, the same as they always do, yet without despoiling colonies, by making nuclei to keep them in from the time they were hatcht till they commenced to lay. My first plan was to take virgin queens from eight to ten days old, into the fields to places where I believed that drones congregated, by the loud roaring which I heard in high altitudes, between the hours of 1 and 3 o'clock p. m.

I would then let them out of the wire-cloth cages which I had carried them in, leaving each one in a separate place, near some old stump or stone, from which they could mark the location of their cage. The queens would mark the place from which they went, the same as they would when coming from a hive, circling farther and farther, till lost from sight. some of them being gone a long time (long enough to meet a drone), when they would return and re-enter the cage, and if I was on hand they could be easily secured again; but I have to report only failure along this line. If allowed to do as they pleased, after returning they would fly out again and again, till they would finally go off, never to return.

My next plan was to take a very few young bees and a little piece of comb in these cages, but with this I was no more successful. Why no queen should ever come back under such circumstances, bearing the marks of fertilization, is more than I can understand, yet such has always been the case.

Through the suggestion of Mr. D. A. Jones, I next tried putting the queen over a hive of bees, keeping her in a double wire-cloth cage, the wire-cloth being so far apart that the bees from the hive below could not reach her, while an entrance was made from the cage to the outside of the hive through a tube. Here the queen would stay, with no apparent desire to go out, any more than she would if she were kept in a queen-nursery till she was too old to become fertilized.

I tried putting a few young bees and a little piece of brood in with them, but in a little while the queen, bees and all, would be gone, only to appear, perhaps, where they would do lots of damage by entering a hive having queen-cells in it, or one having a valuable queen. Then the ants were determined to reside with these isolated queens, as the few bees with them would not keep the ants away, so that, on the whole, the failure in this was even greater than the first, for all were eventually lost.

My next plan was to take the few sections from the hives, which I sometimes found with brood in them, taking bees and all, after which glass sides were put on so as to keep the bees from getting out. They were then carried to the bee-cellar, where they were left one day, when a queen was given them. They were then left till the queen was old enough to become fertilized, when they were put on a shelf on the inside of the shop, near a hole which had been made for them to go out through—a hole being cut through the section to match. In this way I succeeded in getting a number of laying queens; but as these were only nuclei on a very small scale, and as the bees bothered me by going out with the queen, the whole thus becoming lost, I gave it up as a thing not worthy of pursuing farther.

At about this time I saw in some of the bee-papers, that, by accident, a queen had become fertilized in an upper story of a hive workt for extracted honey, the same having a laying queen below, with a queen-excluding honey-board between the upper and lower story, the queen having gone out to meet the drone through an opening which had been left between the upper hive and the queen-excluder. I was not long in seeing where my hobby might now be brought to the desired consummation, so I began experimenting.

I first tried to see if I could get a queen to laying in an upper story, the same as I had read about; so I put some brood "up-stairs," and the next day I gave a queen-cell nearly ready to hatch, the same as I would have done had it been a queenless colony or a nucleus.

In a day or two afterward, I examined the upper story, and found that the queen had hatcht, and apparently as much at home as if she had been in any ordinary colony. In four days more I bored a three-fourths inch hole in the back part of this upper hive, which was left open till the queen commenced to lay, being about the usual time, taking queens as they average.

I expected that the bees would use this hole for an entrance, to some extent at least; but in this I was mistaken, for scarcely a bee was ever seen at the hole, altho a few came out on account of the disturbance when the hole was first put through.

This was late in the fall, but so confident was I of continued success that during the winter I prepared several hives, so that I could slide down a sheet of queen-excluding metal, three and one-half inches from either side, at any time that I wisht during the next season. This space gave ample room for handling the two frames that it was designed to contain, manipulating them the same as I would in a nucleus hive.

When the season for tiering-up arrived, the next year, these hives were put on as upper stories, over queen-excluding honey-boards; and when the colonies became strong enough to fully occupy them, a frame having a little brood was substituted for one of the combs at each end, and the queen-excluding metal placed in the grooves made for it.

I now had in each end of these upper hives, one comb like the rest in the upper story, and one having some brood in it, to which the queen after hatching would be confined, while the bees were at liberty to roam over the whole of both stories of the hive at pleasure.

Into each end of the hive I then placed a queen-cell nearly ready to hatch, pressing it on the comb the same as I have spoken of in a preceding chapter; then I awaited results. The queens in the lower part of these hives were very prolific, the same being selected on purpose, as I desired to try the plan under the most unfavorable circumstances, so as to know if there was any chance of a failure. An examination, two days later, revealed that all of the queens had hatcht and were perfectly at home.

Four days later, a three-fourths inch hole was bored through the back part of the hive near each end, so as to come into the apartment where the queens were confined; while a button made of inch stuff was fixt to turn on a screw, so that when the hole was open the button formed a little alighting-board immediately underneath the hole, and when turned it closed the hole entirely, leaving the hive as tight as it was before. The holes were left open for the next four days, when an examination showed that the queens had commenced to lay; and they were as nice, large queens as I ever saw, when at this stage of their existence.

The buttons were now turned, and the queens left for two days, when they had filled every available cell with eggs—probably to the amount of three-fourths of a frame, as there was considerable honey in the combs. They were now taken out and sent to customers, or used in the apiary, according as I had place for them, when more cells were placed on the combs, and the buttons turned open again six days afterward. In due time I had more laying queens ready to use, and that without hindering the work of the hive a particle, the bees working right along, and the old queen doing duty below, the same as if she was the only queen in the hive. More cells were given again, and so on during the season, success attending every effort.

As hinted at in a former chapter, queens can be fertilized from sections in the same way, by having a little brood in one of them, and enclosing those which the queen is allowed to occupy, with perforated-zinc; but, as I said before, I do not recommend the plan to be used that way. It will work equally well where using half-depth frames, as many do when producing extracted honey; only, to be sure of success, there should be a little brood in one frame or comb.

When I found that my "hobby" was really an actual fact, I felt to rejoice, I assure you; and had it not been that I had resolved to give the matter in book form, these facts (together with how to get the queen-cells built, just when and where they were desired), would have been given to the public long ago.

I find that to get the best results, the holes through which the queens pass when going out to be fertilized, must be on the back part of the hive, or on the opposite side from the entrance; for if on the sides of the hive, or in front, now and then a queen will go to the entrance upon returning from her wedding-tour, and, as the bees are all of the same family, this young queen will be allowed to go in and kill the one reigning below. While experimenting to find out where these queen-entrances should be, I had three queens killed in the lower part of the hive during one season; the last two of which were young queens, having been laying only a month or two.

This is a singular freak, and one which I do not know how to account for; but I do know, that so far every virgin queen that has succeeded in getting from the upper story into the lower one has superseded the queen reigning there, whether that queen was young or old. Why they should think more of a virgin queen than of a laying one, under these circumstances, is the mystery; for in all other cases it is almost impossible to get a colony, having a laying queen, to accept of a virgin, as thousands of bee-keepers are ready to testify.

If it is desired to have more than two queens fertilized from one upper story, it can be done by making more queen apartments with the perforated-zinc, and inserting the cells so that they will hatch at different times, when, by keeping the buttons over the holes where the queens are too young to be fertilized, several can be allowed to go out on the back part of the hive, as they are ready to mate. If many upper stories are used in the apiary probably the plan as I have given it will yield all of the queens required, except for those doing a large business at queen-rearing.

These holes in the upper hive do not materially injure the same, for, if at any time they are wanted to be closed permanently, all we have to do is to cut some plugs of the right size, with a plug-cutter (such as is used by wagon-makers, in cutting plugs to put over the heads of screws), and put them in the holes, when one or two coats of paint will make the hive as good as ever.

By using the above plan, nuclei never need be formed, except by those who want to rear early queens for market, or by those who rear queens by the thousand for sale; in which case more or less nuclei would doubtless have to be made; for we could not get our colonies strong enough for the upper stories, very early in the season, and unless the apiary was a very large one there might be a limit to the upper stories in which to have queens fertilized.

I think no one will deny that the plan as given in this book, of rearing queens at pleasure, and having them fertilized in the same hive with a laying queen, is quite a step in advance of what we were 25 years ago, in this part of our beloved pursuit. The doing of this, without in the least interfering with the working of any colony, must, it seems to me, commend itself to every apiarist.

CHAPTER XIV.

BEE-FEEDERS AND BEE-FEEDING.

In all of the work of queen-rearing it is essential, if we would produce good queens, to feed the queen-rearing colonies when honey is not coming in from the fields, whether the queens are reared in upper stories or in queenless colonies; even where a frame of prepared cells is placed in a colony which is preparing to swarm (as I frequently do in the swarming season, when conducting new experiments), the bees will do nothing with them, unless they are getting sweets from some source.

Many, undoubtedly, have bee-feeders of their own which they think work well, and no doubt they do in general feeding, for at such times almost any feeder will answer; but for feeding during queen-rearing I am satisfied that there is no feeder that will compare with the division-board feeder, after having tried nearly every feeder in use. By using this feeder, the food is near the bees, being in the same department with them, and in such way that where even small nuclei are fed there is no more danger of robbing than there would be were so much stores in the comb placed in the hive.

The engraving on page 28 represents one of the division-board bee-feeders now in use, but I prefer one made as follows:

Make a frame, just as you would make one of the frames for a hive, except that for the bottom-bar you are to use a piece of wood one inch thick, and of the same width as the side-bars. In making this feeder, it will be enough better to pay, if the joints are put together with white lead; for, by so doing, there is no danger of its ever leaking.

Having the frame made, nail on each side (nailing quite thickly with wire-nails three-fourths of an inch in length) a piece of one-eighth inch stuff, as wide as the frame is deep, lacking three-fourths of an inch. Having this nailed on, take off the top-bar (which should have been only slightly nailed on at first), and slip down in the centre of the feeder a side-bar of a frame, having previously bored some holes through it, so that the food may flow freely from the side where it is poured, into the opposite side, through this centre-piece. Now nail through the side of the feeder to this side-bar, thus fastening the thin sides to it, so that, should you ever wish to entirely fill the feeder, when doing rapid feeding, the sides would not spring out against the combs.

Next, heat some wax or paraffine quite hot (paraffine is preferred), so that it will penetrate the wood thoroughly, and pour it into the feeder till the same is nearly full, allowing it to remain for about one minute. By this time it will begin to come through the thin sides, thus showing when it should be poured out. In this way, the wood is so filled with paraffine, or wax, that the feeder will never soak up the food so as to become sour. After pouring out the paraffine, when the feeder becomes cold, nail on the top-bar, which should have a hole (of the right size to fit the funnel that you may have) bored through it near one end, to place the funnel in when pouring in the feed.

Now hang the feeder in the hive the same as you would any frame, only let it be next to one side or the other of the hive, touching the same, so that the bees cannot go on the rear side of it. Here it can be always left, unless you want it out, for some reason. The reason for placing it close to the side of the hive is, that less heat will be wasted in this way than otherwise, and that the bees will have no loafing-place behind it, should you ever want to leave it in full colonies.

Whatever is used to cover the hive (whether honey-board enameled cloth, or a quilt), should have a hole in it to match the hole in the feeder. I prefer to use enameled-cloth, as it is always removed easily, during the many manipulations which must be performed, with any colony that is rearing queens. Then all we have to do to feed, when such cloth is used, is to cut a slit in it over the hole in the top-bar of the feeder, through which the end of the funnel can be inserted. When the funnel is removed, the hole closes up so as to exclude all bees, besides keeping the warmth in, which is also quite an advantage. If a honey-board is used, then a little block must be provided to place over the hole.

In feeding, I use a common watering-pot, minus the "rose" (such as is used in watering plants), to carry the food in. This will hold about 25 pounds of food, and is fixt so that I may know just how many pounds I feed each colony at one time, and so that I can feed as little, or as much, as I choose. To do this, I pour the food into the vessel on the scales, and when the scales indicate one pound in it, I stop pouring, and mark the vessel in three equi-distant places, just at the top of the food; when another pound is poured in, and the vessel markt as before. In this way I keep on until the top is reacht, when the food is poured out, the vessel washt and dried, after which a fine line of paint is put over each mark on the tin. At the end of the first line at the bottom, the figure one is placed; at the next, the figure two, and so on, placing the figure at the end of each mark, till I reach the top. I let this paint become thoroughly dry, when I have something that will be a permanent register of the number of pounds of food that I have in the vessel at any time, when the vessel stands upright.

I now put in 10, 15, 20 or more pounds of food in the vessel, according as I want to feed, and go to the bee-yard. If I desire to feed a colony one pound, I notice where the syrup stands, and, after inserting the funnel in the feeder, I pour in what I judge to be a pound, when the vessel is allowed to hang in an upright position, and at a glance I can tell how nearly right I was.

After a little practice one becomes so accustomed to this matter, that it will be a rare thing that a second pouring is needed. If I want to feed but one-half pound, I can arrive at this close enough, by dividing the space between the marks, with the eye; if more than a pound, count off the marks, pour in the food till it comes to the mark desired, and the work is done, without any fussing or guessing about the amount that has been fed.

As bees do better work at cell-building when the colony building them is getting honey liberally, I prefer to feed these colonies quite heavily at times when no honey is com-ing in from the fields; and when I find a nucleus that needs feeding, I do this by exchanging one of its combs for a full one, from one of these queen-rearing colonies. In this way I keep the food out of the way of these colonies, feed them as they should be fed while cell-building, and feed the nuclei, all at the same time.

As the feeder is always in the hive handy, and the scale which marks off the food is always with me when I go to feed, I think that it is the easiest and best way that feeding can be done.

It will also be seen that if a robber-bee tries to procure

food out of this feeder, it must pass up through the cluster of bees, to the top of the hive, then down into the feeder, before it can get to the food, which practically excludes robbing from this source. -

When queen-rearing is carried on after the honey-harvest is over in the fall, queens are slow to become fertilized, and the later in the season it is, the more loth to go out they become. In such cases it is necessary to feed the nuclei a little, so as to stimulate the bees into activity, which will cause the queens to fly when they otherwise would not. One-fourth pound of food, poured into the feeders of nuclei having queens old enough to be fertilized, will bring them out every time, if poured in at about 11 a. m. On all other occasions, I advise feeding just at night, but it will do to feed in the forenoon in this case; for, let the little colonies get excited as much as they will, there are not enough bees in each hive to get on a rampage, as does a strong colony.

CHAPTER XV.

SECURING GOOD DRONES.

It is my belief that we as apiarists of the Nineteenth Century do not look to the high qualities of our drones as much as we ought, or as much as we do to these qualities in our queens. To me, it seems that the matter of good drones is of greater value, if possible, than is that of good queens; for I believe that the father has as much, or more, to do with the impress left on the offspring than does the mother. We select our queens with great care, but leave them to mate with drones of a promiscuous rearing from all of the colonies in our bee-yard, as well as with the "scrubs" reared by our neighbors, or from such swarms as may be in the woods near us. Now this ought not so to be; for if we would have the best of bees, our queens must mate with the best of drones.

To this end, it seemed to me that one of the most desirable things possible about queen-rearing, would be the fertilizing of queens in confinement. For this reason I have tried every plan given to the public, for the accomplishment of this object, but, as I said in a previous chapter, I have so far nothing to record but failures. I would willingly

give $500 for a plan by which I could mate the queens that
I rear, to selected drones as I wish, and do this with the
same ease and assurance that our other work about the
apiary is carried on.

As we cannot as yet, do this, I find that the next best
thing that I can do, is to set apart two or three of my very
best queens for drone-rearing, causing them, as far as may
be, to rear all of the drones in the apiary. I do this by giving these colonies a large amount of drone-comb, and keeping up their strength, if need be, by giving them worker-
brood from other colonies.

The other colonies are largely kept from rearing drones,
by allowing only worker-combs in their hives, and by giving
them a comb of drone-brood occasionally from one of the
colonies rearing drones, just when they want drones the
most; for if this is not done, they will have drones anyway,
even if they have to tear down worker-comb to build such
as is needed to rear them in. As soon as the major part of
the drones from this comb have hatcht, it is taken away,
before the inferior drone-brood (if any is placed in the
comb) has time to mature. In this way I get all the drones
reared from my best queens, and only fail in not being able
to sort out the weak and feeble ones, or, in not being able
to select the most robust drones for the queens.

To be sure, we can use the drone-traps now before the
public, to keep the drones of the poorer colonies from flying; but to me, this causes more work and more disturbance with the bees than the plan outlined.

Again, the rearing of drones causes a great consumption
of honey, and it seems foolish to be wasting honey in rearing drones only for the sake of killing them after we have
them reared.

Beside knowing how to rear mostly good drones, we
want to know how to get them early in the spring. This is
something not often spoken of, but it is one of the things
which must be done by the queen-rearer who would please
his customers. To do this, I place drone-comb in the centre
of the hives having my drone-rearing queens, doing this in
the fall, so that whenever the bees have any desire for
drones, such comb will be handy for the queen.

If these colonies are not very strong in the spring, I
make them so by giving hatching brood from other colonies
till they are running over with bees, while in addition to
this I often insert a drone-comb full of honey, right in the
centre of the brood-nest; for in the removing of a part of
all this honey, the bees coax the queen to lay in this drone-
comb to a degree that otherwise could not be attained.

In this way I usually succeed in getting drones from one to three weeks earlier than I otherwise would.

To keep drones late in the fall, I make a strong colony queenless at the close of the honey-harvest, and in this colony I put all of the drone-brood that I can find in my drone-rearing colonies at this time. As much of this brood is in the egg and larval form, when given to the queenless colony, I have them hatching after all the other drones are killed off, for queenless colonies which are strong are very choice of drone-brood. In this way I generally have a hive full of nice drones as late as I desire to rear queens, keeping them frequently into October.

As soon as I am through with such drones, I introduce a queen to the colony, when the bees will destroy them at once, if feeding is withheld. I always feed a colony keeping drones when honey is not coming in, for they need much food to make them fly freely, and that is what we want them to do on every warm day at that season of the year.

One other item that I wish to notice at some length, before closing this chapter on drones, is this: From the fact that worker-bees can lay eggs that will hatch drones, and that virgin queens can also lay eggs which will also produce drones, the theory has obtained very largely among bee-keepers that the drones from a fertile queen must of necessity be of the same blood as they would have been had this queen produced drones before she was fertilized. In nearly every book written on bees, that I have read, where this subject is toucht upon, we find words to the effect that, "a pure queen, however mated, must produce a pure drone of her own variety." Mr. Alley's "Queen-Rearing" is an exception to this, I am happy to note.

Now I am not prepared to say how, nor wherein, the drones are changed by the mating of the queen; but this I do know, that drones are contaminated, to a certain extent, by the mating of a queen of one blood with a drone of another blood. Any one can prove this, for in four generations, by mating the queen each time to these pure (?) drones, a bee can be produced which no man can tell from a hybrid. That this contamination does not show in the first cross, is the reason, I believe, that the theory has been accepted, by nearly all, as the truth.

To illustrate: Take a pure black queen, and after she has mated with a fine, yellow Italian drone, let her rear all of the drones produced in an apiary containing only black bees. Of course, the drones from this queen will all be black to look at, the same as they would have been had she mated with a drone of the same blood as herself. Now rear queens in this apiary, from any of the pure black mothers in it, and these young queens will mate with the drones from this mismated queen. These young queens will apparently produce all black workers and drones, the same as they would have done had these drones come from a pure black mother, mated with a pure black drone; but when we rear queens from these young mothers, now and then one will show a little yellow, which would not have been seen, had not the drones from this mismated queen been the least bit contaminated. To detect any slight contamination of blood in our bees, we must always look to the queen progeny, for the queen is the typical bee of the hive; hence they will show an impurity where the workers and drones would not.

Now, take one of these young virgin queens showing a little yellow, and have her mated with a pure yellow Italian drone—the same as was done with the first queen. From this one rear all of your drones again, while you rear queens from her mother, which young queens would be sisters to the one now producing drones. Having one of these last young queens fertilized by the desired drones, next rear queens from her, and you will find that some of these queens will show quite a little yellow on them; yet so far the drones and workers show little if any difference.

Take one of the yellowest queens from this last lot, and have her mated with a yellow drone again, going over the same process of mating as before, and you will get queens in this third generation which will (many of them) be quite yellow; while the workers and drones will show "yellow blood" about them by occasional "splotches" of that color.

Now follow out the same line of breeding once more, and you will get both workers and drones, which any queen-breeder in the land will call hybrids—calling them rightly so, too. These hybrids could not possibly come about by this way of breeding, only as drones from a mismated queen are contaminated; for so far we have used no drones except those which were pure black, according to the parthenogenesis theory, yet we have a hybrid bee as the result.

Worker-bees and drones do not show a little variation of purity, as much as does the queen, hence if we would know of the stock which we have, we must rear queens from them. Failing to do this, we often decide that we have pure drones for breeding purposes, because these same drones look all right.

If I have made this matter plain, and I think that I have, it will be seen how much value it would be to the scientific breeder of queens, if he could select just the drone he wanted, and then have a valuable virgin queen mated with that drone. In this way we could accomplish as much in securing the "coming bee," in two years, as we now accomplish in a life-time.

Let no one be longer deceived about pure drones from a mismated queen; for if such drones are allowed to fly in your yard you cannot expect any satisfactory degree of purity from queens reared therein. I have been forced to this conclusion by many carefully-conducted experiments, as already described.

CHAPTER XVI.

THE INTRODUCTION OF QUEENS.

Perhaps there is no one subject connected with bee-keeping that has received so much notice in our bee-papers and elsewhere, as has the introduction of queens; yet all who have read the methods and discussions given, must have plainly seen that success does not always attend the efforts in this direction. On the contrary, many losses have been reported, and these losses are not confined to the inexperienced altogether, for we often hear of our most practical apiarists occasionally losing a queen.

The reason for so many losses, it seems to me, arises from the fact that bee-keepers in general do not understand that a discrimination should be made between queens taken from one hive and placed in another, and those which have come long distances by mail or express. In introducing queens, it should always be borne in mind that a queen taken from one hive in the apiary, and introducing into another, does not require one-half the care that must be given to a queen coming from a distance. The reason for this seems to be, that a queen taken from a hive in the same yard, is still heavy with eggs, and will not run around, provoking the bees to chase her, as will a queen after having had a long journey.

In introducing all ordinary queens coming from my own apiary, I generally adopt one of the two following plans:

The first is, to go to a nucleus or other hive from which I wish to get a queen, and when she is found I take the frame of brood she is on, bees and all, together with another frame from the same hive, carrying them to the hive from which I am to take the superannuated queen, when they are left with the queen between the two combs, while I secure the poor queen and dispose of her; then I take out two frames from this hive, and place the two frames, brought from the nucleus, in their places, and close the hive. I now shake off the bees from the two frames in front of their own hive, carrying the combs to the nucleus; or if the nucleus will be too weak, I carry bees and all to it.

The object in taking the two frames with the queen, is so that while waiting outside of the hive she and the most of the bees may cluster between them, thus becoming quiet. When placed in the hive, both are put in together, thus leaving the queen quiet among her own bees. In this way I do not lose one queen out of fifty, and as the operation is so simple, and the queen so quickly installed, the advantages more than over-balance so small a loss.

The second plan is to go to any nucleus and get the young queen in a round wire-cloth cage (such as all bee-keepers have in their apiaries) before looking for the queen to be superseded. After she is in the cage, I place her in my pocket, and close the hive that I took her from, and look for the queen that I wish to remove; having found her, she is killed or otherwise taken care of, and this hive is also closed. I next blow in at the entrance enough smoke to alarm the whole colony, pounding with my fist on top of the hive until I hear a loud roaring inside, which shows that the bees are filling themselves with honey. I now let the queen that I have in the cage run in at the entrance, smoking her as she goes in, while I still keep pounding on the hive. In doing this, nothing but wood-smoke should be used, for if tobacco-smoke were used many of the bees would be suffocated.

If this is done, when there is danger of robbing, I wait till just at night about the operation. If more convenient, the queen can be taken out of the hive at any time during the day, and the operation of putting in the new queen done just at night. Some seem to think that the operation will be more successful if done in this way, but so far I fail to see any difference as to results. The idea is to cause the bees to fill themselves with honey, at the same time smoking them so that the queen and bees smell alike. This plan is as free from loss as the other, still it is not quite so simple as the first—I only adopt it where it is not handy to use the former.

Where any colony has been queenless from three to five

days, a queen can generally be successfully introduced by dropping her in honey, and rolling her over in the same till she is thoroughly daubed with it, when the cover to the hive is lifted, and the queen dropt from a spoon right down among the bees. This is equally successful with the others, but I do not like the plan, on account of having to keep the colony queenless so long. Even a queen coming from a distance can generally be safely introduced by this plan.

To introduce a queen that has come to me from abroad, or one which I consider of more than ordinary value from my own apiary, I proceed as follows: First, I take the cage containing the queen and her escort of bees to the little room where I handle queen-cells, and open the cage before the window, so that if the queen takes wing she will not be lost. I then catch the queen and clip her wings (as given in the chapter on that subject), when she is placed in a round, wire-cloth cage; but I allow none of her escort to go with her, as I consider such bees when left with a queen one of the prime causes of the many losses which occur to the purchaser of queens.

Having the queen's wings clipt, and in the cage, I next take a piece of wire-cloth, containing 14 to 16 meshes to the inch, and cut it four-and-one-half by eight-and-one-half inches in size. Now cut a piece three-fourths of an inch square out of each corner, and bend the four sides at right angles, so as to make a box, as it were, three inches wide by seven inches long, and three-fourths of an inch deep. Next, unravel the edges down one-half way, so that the points can be pressed into the combs, and if the corners do not stay together as they should, they can be sewed together with one of the wires which were unraveled (Fig. 5, page 35).

Having the cage ready, and the queen to be introduced, in your pocket, proceed to look for the queen to be replaced. and after removing her, examine the combs until you find one from which the bees are just hatching, or where you can see them gnawing at the cappings of the cells, which comb should also have some honey along the top-bar of the frame above the hatching brood.

Now shake and brush every bee off this comb, and place on it the queen that you have in your pocket, by putting the open end of the cage near the comb over some cells of unsealed honey, when she will go to the comb, and as soon as she comes to the honey she will begin eating. While she is doing this, put the large cage over her and the hatching brood, as you wish, taking all of the time that is needed, for as long as she continues eating she will not go away, nor be disturbed by any of your motions.

Having honey in the cage is necessary, for the bees outside of the cage cannot be depended upon to feed a queen when she is being introduced. Some claim that if the cage is made of wire-cloth having large meshes, the bees will feed them; but after losing many queens by depending upon the bees to care for them, I say always provision your introducing-cage in some way, so that the queen is not dependent upon the bees for her food while in the cage.

Even when keeping queens in the queen-nursery, where placed in queenless colonies, I find that the bees often refuse to feed them; so I now provision all cages of all kinds, notwithstanding the claim put forth by some of our best bee-keepers that several caged fertile queens will be fed by a colony having a laying queen, if they are put between the combs in a hive having such, for safe keeping. Finding a whole queen-nursery full of dead queens, after trusting them to the care of a colony of bees having a laying queen, is generally more convincing than many words given in support of an untruthful theory.

But to return: Fit the cage so that it comes over three or four square inches of honey, and as much of the hatching brood as possible; for these hatching bees have much to do with the speedy introduction of the queen. Having all fixed, leave the hive from 12 to 48 hours, according as your other work will allow you, when the hive is to be opened and the cage examined.

If all has workt as it usually does, the bees will be found spread out evenly over the cage, the same as they are on any of the rest of the combs. When such is the case, the cage is to be carefully lifted from over the queen, letting her and the young bees that have hatcht during her confinement, go where they please, keeping watch all the while to see that the bees treat her kindly; if they do this (as they will nineteen times out of twenty), the comb is to be placed in the hive; if not, she is caged again. In from one-half to one hour after liberating her, look at the queen again, and if she is now treated as their old queen was before her removal, the hive is closed and she is considered safely introduced.

If, on the contrary, the bees are found clustered thickly on the cage, biting the wire-cloth and showing signs of anger, the frame is to be placed back in the hive and left till the next day, when, if they still show the same symptoms, you must wait until they are scattered over the cage, as spoken of at first, before letting her out.

I often release a queen in 12 hours, and find that she is all right; and I rarely have to wait to let her out, more than 24 hours. Still, in extreme cases, I have been obliged to keep them caged nearly or quite ten days.

Do not be afraid of the queen dying in the cage; for if she is placed over honey, as I have advised, she will live a month, and there is no need of losing any queen if there is not too much haste used in letting her out. Even then there should be no danger, if the apiarist is on hand to release the queen from the bees which cluster (or ball) her, as they always do a queen for some time before they kill her. Such clustered queens can easily be releast, by smoking the bees till they free her.

In liberating a queen from a "ball" of infuriated bees, she is liable to take wing and fly away, thus losing her in that way. To guard against this, I either clip her wings before trying to introduce her, or take the "ball" of bees into a room while smoking them apart. Again, there is some danger that after the queen is free, a bee from the cluster will sting her, if this bee gets to the queen singly; and for this reason I always secure the queen in a wire-cloth cage as soon as the last bee has let go of her.

If the bees of any hive have once clustered a queen, I find that it is very hard work to get them to accept the same one afterward; for this reason I generally take a queen that has been clustered, to some other hive and introduce her there, giving the infuriated colony another queen or a queen-cell.

However, not one queen in one hundred is treated in this way when using the above plan, for, as a rule, I find that the young bees that have hatcht in the cage with her, have accepted this queen as their mother; thus the news is conveyed from them to the rest of the bees in the hive, so that she is fed by "all hands," which causes her to keep the cells enclosed by the cage from which the young bees have hatcht well supplied with eggs.

After the queen has been laying eggs for one or two days, she is as safe as if she had been reared in the hive; and for this reason I do not liberate the queen till I see eggs in the cells enclosed by the cage, unless it is in the fall of the year after queens have ceast laying.

At this time of the year (fall) I am in no hurry to liberate a queen, for she is of no especial use out among the bees when she is not laying eggs, hence I generally leave them in the cage for a week or two, until I know that the

bees will accept of the queen after I take the cage from
over her, without further trouble. Now there are no bees
hatching from the combs, so in caging the queen I only see
that she is in the centre of the cluster, and has plenty of
honey to eat inside of the cage; for when a queen is not
laying she has to help herself to honey the same as any
other bee.

In using these cages, the comb next to them should be
left a bee-space from the cage, so that the bees can go all
around it, thus getting acquainted with the new queen much
more quickly than they otherwise would. If this space cannot be procured in any other way, one frame should be left
out of the hive for the time being.

The advantage that this plan has over any other where
the queen is to be caged in the hive, is in the young bees
hatching out in the cage with the queen; and as they have
known no other mother, they accept her at once, thus forming an escort which the older bees, sooner or later, are
obliged to accept as being a part and parcel of the colony.

By any of the foregoing plans there is very little danger
of losing a queen, yet none of them are absolutely safe;
nor would I use them were I to receive a very valuable
queen, say one worth $10, for with such queens we do not
wish to take a particle of risk.

After studying on the method of forming nuclei by the
"caged bees" plan, as I gave in the chapter on that subject,
I saw that by using that process I had an absolutely safe
plan of introducing a laying queen, even were she worth
$100. I have used this plan with all the valuable queens
for several years, and have not lost a single queen, nor do
I believe that I ever shall lose one by it, unless she should
happen to fly away in putting her in the box with the bees;
nor will she do this as long as I clip all of my queens'
wings.

My usual method of using this plan, is to get bees
enough from the upper stories of different hives to form a
good, strong colony, doing it just the same as I gave in the
chapter on forming nuclei, only I take the bees out of four
or five different hives, and off from ten to fifteen combs,
according to the strength that I want the colony. After
having the bees in the box, they are treated just the same as
there described, giving them the valuable queen in the same
way that the virgin queen was given.

In hiving them, give as many empty combs, or combs of
honey, as you choose, but do not give any more brood at
this time than you did to the nucleus; for if more brood is
given, the bees sometimes will swarm out with the queen in

a few days, where made so strong, the same as a natural swarm. If you desire to give brood, do it by giving a frame or two at one time every few days, after waiting four or five days from the time of hiving before giving the first frames.

If you do not have bees in upper stories having a queen-excluder under them, then go to two or three colonies in ordinary hives, look for the queens, and as fast as they are found put the frames that they are on outside of the hives. Now smoke and jar the bees on two or three frames from each hive, till they fill themselves with honey, when you are to shake as many bees down through the funnel into the box as you want in your colony, and proceed as before.

If you desire to introduce the queen to a certain colony, (the same as we have been doing by the other plans given), kill or take away the old queen and cause the bees to fill themselves with honey the same as in the last instance; when all the bees that you can get are to be shaken off the combs through the funnel into the box.

Having all of the bees in the box that you can possibly obtain, treat them the same as before until you are ready to hive them. After they are placed in the cellar or other cool place, take all of the combs having brood in them, and give them to the other colonies, leaving one or two frames of honey in the hive to hold till night the bees which you did not succeed in getting into the box and those returning from the fields. These combs should be put in the centre of the hive, so that when night comes the bees will be mostly clustered on them instead of about the side of the hive, as would be the case if they were left next to one side of the hive. When you hive the bees having the new queen with them, take these two combs with the bees out of the hive, putting in other combs as before, using only one having a little brood in it, and that taken from another hive, so that they are not given their own brood.

Having all prepared, proceed to hive the bees as was done with the nucleus; or, if preferred, the bees can be shaken down at the entrance, for, as this is their old home, they can go nowhere else even should they try to do so. After the larger part of the bees are in the hive, shake the bees off from the two combs and let them run in with the others. In five days commence to give the brood back again, and keep on doing so occasionally until all is back in the hive as it was before.

The above I believe to be an infallible plan for introducing queens, and well pays for the time and trouble, when we have a very valuable queen coming from a distance, which we would not lose on any account; yet it will hardly pay to spend so much time on ordinary queens, except by way of experiment, or when desiring to make new colonies in addition to introducing queens. Where a queen comes to me very unexpectedly, I always use this plan, taking the bees from an upper story or two, thus forming a small colony with the queen, which colony is built up later on by giving frames of hatching brood. Using it in this way it always gives me the assurance of success in any case of emergency.

CHAPTER XVII.

INTRODUCING VIRGIN QUEENS.

That just-hatcht virgin queens which are so young as to be white, weak and fuzzy, can be introduced to any colony that will accept a sealed queen-cell, is a fact known to all; and if there was no need of ever introducing virgin queens older than these, this chapter would never have been written.

However, in these days of progress, and of close competition in the queen traffic, it is very desirable to have some plan whereby we can introduce a virgin queen from five to eight days old, to a nucleus, as soon as a laying queen is taken away from it; as well as to introduce one into any other colony where we wish to place a virgin queen coming to us from a distance, which we have ordered to improve our stock by a direct cross between her and one of our drones. From the fact that not one colony in 500 will take such a virgin queen, when giving her at the time of taking away the laying one, comes the reason that such a plan of safe introduction will be of greater value to us than it would be could we succeed in introducing these queens as well as we can a laying queen.

On no one thing in bee-keeping have I spent so much thought as on how to successfully introduce virgin queens from four to ten days old; and I am happy to say that I am master of the situation; not that I have dug it out all alone, for I have not. I have pickt up little things here and there for several years, and by saving every little item that proved to be in advance of what I already had, and applying them, together with what I could study out myself, eventually gave me success.

As I said in the preface, I cannot give credit to all from whom I have gained knowledge, for I have not tried to keep the authors of all these things in mind; besides, there has been scarcely a writer in the past, who has written for our bee-papers, from whom I have not gained some light; so if I were to single out some I would do injustice to others. I claim very little as original with myself, and I am glad to know that it is the "littles" of the past, coming from the thousands who have engaged in our pursuit, that have made the "mickle" of the present; hence very few are able to say, "I am more holy than thou."

My first ideas in this matter came from the need of procuring a laying queen from a nucleus more often than could possibly be done by the old plan of giving the nucleus a queen-cell 24 hours after taking a laying queen away from it, in order to overcome the low prices to which queens had fallen, owing to the close competition in this branch of our industry. If a five-days-old virgin queen could be introduced into a nucleus so that she would commence to lay in five days from the time the other was removed, two queens could be taken from one nucleus during the same time we had formerly taken one. All know that by the old plans a laying queen cannot be taken from a nucleus oftener than once in 10 or 12 days.

This one item alone I considered worth striving for; but when it came to be fully understood that it was an object for us as apiarists to change the blood in our stock by a direct cross as often as possible, so as to give greater life and vigor to our bees, then such introduction of oldish virgin queens became almost a necessity. Since this idea was first advanced it has gained ground rapidly in the minds of our best bee-keepers; and I believe that the day is not far distant when the traffic in virgin queens will assume greater proportions than at the present. A virgin queen is not fit to start on a journey until she is at least 24 hours old; and as from 2 to 4 days must be required in her transit, none of the plans of introducing young virgin queens would work in this case.

Without taking the reader over much of the ground which led to the discovery of a plan for the safe introduction of virgin queens, I will give the three plans which I employ—using them according to the circumstances which I am placed under, as to the number of virgin queens on hand, length of time the nucleus or colony has been queenless, etc.

Some 10 or 12 years ago I had a colony rearing queens, that had a nice lot of queen-cells just sealed, when one day a virgin queen escaped from me and flew out of sight. I waited for her to come back, but as she did not I concluded that she was lost. Upon going to get my queen-cells when it was time for them to hatch, I found the cells all torn down, and the queen that I had lost was in the hive just commencing to lay.

Here I was shown that a colony that had been queenless long enough to have their queen-cells capt, would accept a virgin queen under almost any condition. In fact, I had read of this before, but nothing convinces us as does something which comes close at home, to ourselves or our family Through this loss of cells, which occurred just when I needed them very much, came something of great value to me, which I might not have fully known had I not lost them.

From this, I found that whenever I came across a nucleus or colony having queen-cells sealed, all that I had to do to introduce a queen was to go to my queen-nursery and pick out a nice virgin queen and drop her in some honey; when, after pouring some of the honey out of a tea-spoon on her back, and rolling her about in it until she was thoroughly daubed, the quilt was raised from over the frames, and after scooping her up together with some of the honey, I turned the whole down among the bees between the combs. The hive was then closed, and I would usually have a laying queen in three or four days. To prevent the queen from flying, when introducing her in this way, I held the mouth of the cage close down to the honey (which I generally take in a tea-cup), when, by a sudden jar, caused by striking the cage, she was thrown down into the honey, thus daubing her wings, after which there was no further danger.

This plan I also use when receiving a virgin queen from abroad, if I have a colony that has been queenless long enough to have cells sealed. Of course we do not expect many colonies in this condition, but all queen-rearers, as well as apiarists in general, have more or less of them coming from an unexpected loss of queens.

The second plan is one that I use with younger virgin queens—say those from one to three days old—and in all cases where it is not convenient to use either the first or third. It is as follows:

Make a round wire-cloth cage, about an inch in diameter and three-and-one-half inches long. Into one end of this fit a permanent stopper, and for the other saw off a piece of an old, soft-wood broom-handle, five inches long. Whittle one end so that it will go into the cage one-half an inch, when a five-eighths inch hole is to be bored through it lengthwise. Now fill this hole with "Good" candy, made of granulated sugar and honey, packing it in with a plunger quite tightly. Next, put the virgin queen into this cage, and put in the provisioned stopper.

When you go to remove the laying queen, take the cage along with you, and after having removed her and replaced the frames in the hive, lay the cage lengthwise between the top-bars of the two frames having the most brood in them. Put a quilt over all, and close the hive.

As it takes the bees about four days to burrow through, or dig out, the five inches of candy, they become pretty well acquainted with their loss and the existing state of affairs; hence they are ready to accept the queen when she is set at liberty by the removal of the candy. In about eight days time (counting from when the cage was laid on the frames), I generally find this queen laying, without having to open the hive, except as I do it to take out laying queens.

Right here I wish to say, that the cage here described is just such an one as I use about the apiary for all general purposes, except that when so using it I put in a piece of corn-cob for a stopper instead of the one filled with candy.

The third plan, and the only one that I know of that is absolutely safe at all times (for I sometimes have a loss with either of the other two) is as follows:

Get out a little block two inches long by one inch square, through which is to be bored a five-eighths inch hole, boring the same through the block lengthwise. This is to be the base of the cage. Next bore a one-half inch hole through the centre, so as to cross the five-eighths inch hole. Now get two pieces of frame-stuff, four inches long by one inch wide, and one-fourth of an inch thick, boring a five-eighths inch hole in each, near one end, to correspond with the five-eighths inch hole which was bored lengthwise through the little block. Having these ready, nail one to each end of the little block, so that the holes bored in them will match the hole in the block, thus making one continuous hole straight through.

Next get a piece of wire-cloth, eight inches long by two-and-one-half inches wide, and nail it to the frame-stuff and lower edge of the block, so as to form a cage three inches deep by two inches wide and one inch thick, through which the bees can become acquainted with the queen. Now drive

two three-fourths inch wire-nails into the edges of the
frame-stuff, driving one into each piece and letting it project one-fourth of an inch, or, in other words, do not drive
them up to within one-fourth of an inch. With a pair of
cutting pliers, cut off the heads of each nail, and file them to
a sharp point, so that you can fasten the cage on the side
of the hive, or to whatever you like, by simply pressing
these points into the wood.

The cage is now ready for use. To use it, first put the
virgin queen into the cage by letting her run through the
half-inch hole down into it, when a long stopper is put into
the hole to keep her from returning. Now proceed to fill
the five-eighths inch hole with the "Good" candy, as used
in the shipping-cages (this made of powdered sugar instead
of granulated, as will be explained further on), putting it
in at both ends, and pressing it around the long stopper
down in the centre. When this is done, remove the stopper
and fill the place where it came from with more of the
candy, when the cage and queen is ready for the hive.

Next, take a frame having only a starter of foundation
in it, and the caged queen, and proceed to the hive where
you wish to take away a laying queen; after having caught
her, take all of the frames out of the hive and stick the
cage on the side of the hive where you want it, by pressing
it against the wood. Now put in the frame with the foun-
dation-starter and adjust the division-board, closing the
hive. Next, shake all of the bees off the combs near the
entrance, letting them run in, and give these combs to
another colony to care for. They are now to be left for four
or five days, when you will find a laying queen (providing
the queen was four or five days old when put into the cage),
and also the frame partly-filled with worker-comb, in which
the queen has laid.

At times when no honey is coming in, the bees are to be
fed what they need every night, so as to place them in the
same condition that they would be were honey coming in
from the fields. To thus feed, I place a division-board
feeder in the hive, fastening the caged queen to that instead
of to the hive; or, if preferred, the cage can be fastened to
the division-board.

The candy is placed in the block, and the different holes
made in it so that the bees may be good-natured when
coming to the queen; and also to keep the bees from liberating the queen till they have given up all hopes of getting
their laying queen or brood back again, for they would
kill her at once if she was liberated sooner.

It generally takes the bees from 8 to 12 hours to eat

out the candy, being about the time needed to get them reconciled to their new situation. If preferred, the cage ·described in the second plan can be used instead of this one, by cutting off the provisioned stopper to one inch in length; but the last gives a little better satisfaction, inasmuch as the bees have a larger surface of wire-cloth to cluster upon, and they can be eating candy at several places at once, hence they do not rush into the cage so fast when an opening is made into it.

If the queen was not given to the bees when the combs were taken away, many, if not all of them, would go to other hives; for altho the bees do not like her at first, yet she holds them where they belong, as they consider her better than nothing. Do not give them back their brood till the queen begins laying, for if you do they will at once kill the queen, or "hug" her till she is nearly or quite spoiled; for in nothing are bees so determined as they are not to accept of a virgin queen five or more days old, immediately after having their mother taken from them.

When the queen commences to lay, take out the partly-filled frame and give back the combs that you took away from the bees at first, allowing this queen to stay in the hive a few days before you try the operation with the same colony again; for if you keep right on giving virgin queens and taking laying ones out, the colony will soon decline, on account of no young bees hatching to take the place of the old ones which are dying all the while. Young bees could be shaken in the hive every little while if it was preferred to giving back the combs, and in this way a laying queen could be taken from a hive every five days. Of course, where this plan is used with virgin queens coming from abroad, the brood will be put back to remain, as we will desire to keep the queen.

If the colony is other than a nucleus, we shall want to give two or three frames with starters of foundation, so as to give the colony the room they need. These partly-filled frames are used to advantage during the swarming season for new swarms, so that a colony treated in this way is doing valuable work all this time, besides getting our virgin queens fertilized.

I have never lost a queen in this way, no matter if she was 12 days old when placed in the cage; and I consider it an absolutely safe plan for introducing virgin queens, and one of great benefit to those who desire to improve their stock by a direct crossing of queens and drones; but for the purpose of getting queens fertilized in nuclei, oftener than by the old plans, I doubt if it pays, on account of the large amount of work which it requires.

Before leaving the subject of introducing queens I wish to say, that where any plan of introduction is used by which the bees are liable to start queen-cells from their own brood before the introduced queen is liberated, I think that the idea which prevails—that the bee-keeper should look over the combs and destroy all of these cells—is fallacious. All of my experience in this matter proves that a queen will be as quickly accepted when such cells are allowed to remain and when so accepted the bees themselves will destroy the cells. Where I had queen-cells sealed in any colony, I always roll a queen in honey and drop her into the hive, letting the bees attend to the queen-cells when they get ready; and it is a rare thing that I lose a queen by this process, even when such queen is a virgin.

CHAPTER XVIII.

KEEPING A RECORD OF CELLS, QUEENS, ETC.

When I kept but few bees, or reared but few extra queens, I had no trouble in keeping track of what each hive contained; and even where I am working 100 small colonies for queen-rearing, I know what is in each hive in a kind of general way, but not enough so that should I trust to memory many blunders would be made. For this reason, when I began queen-rearing as a business, I found that I must have some way of knowing precisely what was in each hive, so I adopted something to help me in this matter.

The first thing that I used was small, flat stones, four of which were placed under the bottom-board of each hive; so that when an operation was performed with any hive, these stones could be made to tell me very nearly what I wanted to know, from just glancing over the tops of the hives, as some of them were placed in different positions, each time that I workt at the hive, to denote what had been done with it. These stones, together with a piece of section to keep the dates on (the piece of section being placed under the cover of the hive, to keep it from getting wet), does very well, where not over 10 to 20 nuclei are workt.

To use the stones intelligently, we must jot down somewhere what the different positions which the stones occupy indicate, until we get so accustomed to it that our memory is always posted in this matter. For instance: If I look over a hive on June 1, and give the bees a queen-cell, I place one of the stones on the right-hand front corner of

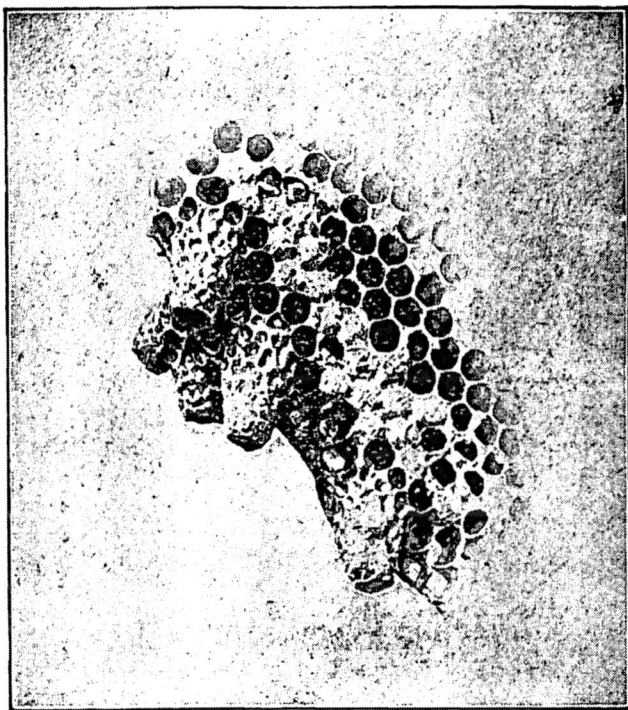

Fig. 11.—A Group of Queen-Cells.

the hive, and put that date on the section. A glance over the yard shows me that all the hives having a stone on that corner had queen-cells placed in them the last thing which I did; and the strip of section will tell me when that was. In the same way when I take out a queen I put this stone on the left-hand front corner, which indicates that the queen from that hive is missing; and when I find a queen-cell hatcht, or a young queen in the hive, this stone is placed on the left-hand back corner, while for a laying queen it is placed on the right-hand back corner, the date being put on the piece of section each time so that the last date shows when the stone was changed, the two together thus telling me all that I wish to know. The main trouble with this plan is that it requires the lifting of the cover to find the date; but as I said at starting, this will answer pretty well where but few colonies are workt for queens.

More of the stones are used to indicate other things. For instance: A stone in the centre of the cover shows that the colony is short of stores and must be fed; while a stone in the centre of the back part of the cover shows that the bees are crowded for room, and that another frame should be given. A stone in the centre of the front indicates that there are too few bees to do good work; and so on, for these stones can be made to tell a great variety of matters.

Again, I use them on all hives workt for honey, having them tell me when the sections were put on, when more room was given, and when taken off; also when the honey was extracted from certain hives, which hives are workt for extracted honey, and which for comb honey, etc. In fact, they are really indispensable to me in working an apiary either for queens or honey, and are in constant use, even when using the cards which are about to be described.

When I first commenced bee-keeping, I had no idea of rearing queens for sale, nor did I think of it until I was crowded into it; so when my first order for a queen came I took the same from a full colony. This queen seemed to give satisfaction, and soon the neighbors of this customer sent for queens, and so on, till I found that I must have a few nuclei to supply this demand for queens which had apparently sprung up of itself. The queens that were reared in partnership, as spoken of in the first chapters, were taken to different apiaries and introduced by myself to colonies at the suggestion of the one who did the rearing, rather than being sent off to customers through the mails.

When the business grew so that I could no longer keep track of it with the stones and pieces of sections to advantage, I secured a sample of "Root's Queen-Registering Cards." These suited me exactly, and they were sold very cheaply. I procured a quantity of them, and have used them ever since. To show the reader what they are, I give a sample card.

QUEEN REGISTER.

No. ....

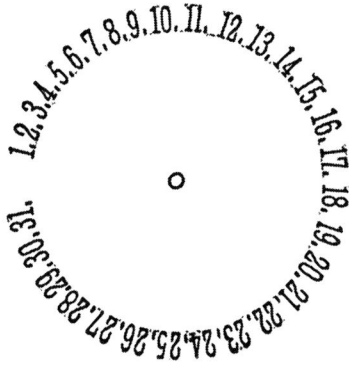

1.2.3.4.5.6.7.8.9.10.11.12.13.14.15.16.17.18.19.20.21.22.23.24.25.26.27.28.29.30.31.

MARCH. APRIL. MAY.

OCT.

SEPT. AUG. JUNE

JULY.

EGGS. **BROOD.**

MISSING. **CELL.**

LAYING. **HATCHED.**

APPROVED.

NOT APPROVED.

DIRECTIONS.—Tack the Card on a conspicuous part of the Hive or Nucleus box; then, with a pair of Pliers, force a common pin into the centre **O** of each circle, after it is bent in such a manner that the head will press securely on any figure or word. Use tinned or galvanized tacks, that will not rust, etc.

It will be seen at a glance that all we have to do after each manipulation with the different hives is to turn the pins to where they tell us just how and when we left the hive when last lookt at, which, together with the stones to tell us about honey, etc., tell all that we want to know.

I have watcht carefully to see if anything better was brought before the public, but so far nothing of the kind has come to my knowledge. These cards are used on the upper stories, the same as on nuclei, using one on each end where two queens are to be fertilized from one hive, and on all hives where a change of queen is made often. No queen-rearing apiary can be complete without something of the kind.

CHAPTER XIX.

CLIPPING THE QUEEN'S WINGS.

Probably there is no other item about bee-keeping on which there is so much diversity of opinion as there is regarding the clipping of queens' wings. Many of our very best apiarists stand directly opposed to others who are equally as good authority. Some claim that the queen is injured by having her wings clipt, and for this reason many are superseded by the bees; while others are equally confident that it is impossible to injure the queen in the least by clipping her wings, if the clipping is delayed, as it always should be, until after the queen has commenced to lay. However, when I look the ground all over, I believe that the greatest number of the "dollar-and-cent apiarists" of our land are on the side of clipping the queens' wings; and as I stand on that side myself, I trust that I shall be excused if I tell the reader in brief some of my reasons for clipping the wings of my queens.

The second year of my bee-keeping life I lost a splendid swarm of bees, being the second swarm that issued from my then small apiary, for I only had one swarm the first year. I felt this loss very keenly, and then and there I resolved that this would be the last one that would ever "run away." In accordance with this resolve, I clipt all of the queens' wings in the yard, and have kept them so ever since, except those that I thought, of late years, I might sell; and altho I now think that resolve a rash one, yet in all of my 20 years of bee-keeping that one swarm has been the only one lost from this cause.

A person can hardly pick up a paper that treats on bees but that he will find an account of swarms going into the woods; and there is no question but what hundreds of dollars' worth of property "took wings and flew away" in just this manner; while if the queens' wings had been clipt this loss might have been saved.

By having the wings of all queens clipt, the bees are perfectly under the control of the apiarist, and he can handle them as he pleases, separating them with pleasure where two or more swarms cluster together, and hive them on the "returning plan" when they come singly. In using this plan, all that we have to do when a swarm issues is to step to the entrance of the hive with a round wire-cloth cage (such as has been described), into which the queen is allowed to run, when the cage is closed up and laid in front of the hive. The old hive is now moved to a new stand, and a hive prepared for a new colony put in its place. In a few minutes the bees miss their queen and come back, running into the hive with fanning wings, when the queen is liberated and goes in with them.

I have followed this plan of hiving bees for years, and I know it to be a good one, as a good yield of honey is generally the result. There is no climbing of trees, cutting off limbs, or lugging a cumbersome basket or swarming-box about. It is so straight-forward, too—remove the old hive to a new stand, put the new hive in its place, and the returning swarm hive themselves without trouble, except the releasing of the queen.

Again, I clip off at least two-thirds of all of the wings of the queen, so that she is always readily found. In making nuclei, changing frames of brood and bees, making swarms, extracting, etc., if you find the queen you can always know that she is just where she belongs, and not in some place where she ought not to be. By having her wings cut short, you can see her golden abdomen as soon as you lift the frame that she is on.

Then the clipping of queens' wings does away with that expense to the apiarist—the fountain pump—or one of some other manufacture, which all apiarists think a necessity where their queens have their wings, so that by the use of it swarms may be kept from clustering together, where two or more come out at once, or if a swarm tries to "run away," so that it can be stopt.

Some claim that a queen with clipt wings is more

liable to fall off the combs and get injured than she would be if her wings were not clipt; but I cannot see how their wings should help them to hold on to the combs as long as that part is done with the feet.

Others claim that unless the apiarist is constantly on hand during the swarming season, many queens will be lost by the bees swarming out and going back, while the queen stays out in the grass, she going so far from the hive that she does not find her way back. If the apiarist is obliged to be away from home, let some one of the family get the queen in the cage, and lay her at the entrance of the hive till the apiarist returns, when he can divide the colony, or let the queen go back, when she will come out with the swarm again the next day. If all are obliged to be away from home, the queens can be readily found upon the return of the apiarist, by his passing through the yard and looking for the queens, which will be found by the little balls of bees from the size of a butternut up to that of an orange; for I have yet to see the queen, thus left in the grass, which did not have this escort of bees with her.

To find the hive that this queen came out of, take the queen away from the bees towards night, when the most of the other bees have stopt flying, and they will return to the hive from which she came, setting up their fanning at the entrance. Now let the queen go in with them, and the swarm will issue again the next day.

If I desire to be gone from home for two or three days together, with my family, I hire a man to stay with the bees from 9 a. m. to 3 p. m., instructing him to cage the queens as they come out with the swarms, and leave them on top of the hive, arranging them in such a way that the bees in the swarm can have access to the cages when they return. Any man can do this, or a boy even, who would not think of hiving swarms. On my return, I liberate these queens, when the swarm will issue again in a day or two; or, if it is preferred, these colonies can be divided.

Still others claim that the bees will swarm out from the new hive with the queen immediately after she has gone, into the hive with the bees; but as far as I can judge, all of these reports come from those who are using so small hives that the bees are not contented with them. In any event, this can be easily overcome by leaving the queen in the cage at the entrance of the hive until the bees have all become quiet, when she is release, with no danger of their coming out in the air again, as has been spoken of.

As to the claim that queens are injured by having their wings clipt, I can only think that such claims are entirely fallacious; for during the past five years I have kept many of my queens with their wings whole (where I thought there might be a call for such queens, which had been wintered over), and not one of them proved in any way superior to those whose wings were clipt. Again, I have had queens sent to me from those who never clip the wings of their queens, and these have shown no superiority over those in my own yard that had their wings clipt.

The clipping of the queen's wings often seems like a serious job to the timid and inexperienced, but after a little practice it is no more of a job than any other work about the apiary. Some recommend scissors for clipping queens' wings, but I think that a queen is much more liable to be injured in using them, by having a leg or two cut off, than where a knife is used.

My way of clipping the wings is as follows: After having found the queen, catch her by the wings, getting all four of them if possible, by using the thumb and fore-finger of the left hand. Now take a jack-knife, which should have one of its blades very sharp, and place the sharpened blade on the wings of the queen. Carefully lower both hands down within an inch or two of the top of the frames, so that the queen will not be injured in falling, when the knife is lightly drawn, the wings severed, and the queen runs unharmed below. In doing this, place the knife so that it will cut off about two-thirds of the wings; for there is no more harm in cutting off this much than there is in cutting off one-half of one wing, as some recommend. By clipping the queen's wings in this way, she is easily found at all times.

Some claim that this destroys the beauty of the queen; but to me it causes her golden abdomen to show off to a much better advantage; and even if it did not, the ease with which they are always found afterward more than compensates for the lack in looks, to those who reason in this way. Do not be afraid of cutting the fingers, for if you stop drawing the knife as soon as the queen drops, you cannot do so.

The best time for clipping queens' wings is during fruit-bloom, when there are but few bees in the hive compared with what there will be later on; doing the same when the bees are industriously working during the middle of the day, so that few are at home.

CHAPTER XX.

SHIPPING, SHIPPING-CAGES, BEE-CANDY, ETC.

Prior to the advent of the Italian bee into this country, the shipping of queens was comparatively unknown, while the sending of queens in the mails is something scarcely a quarter of a century old. In queen-rearing and queen-shipping there have been mighty strides made during the last 25 years—strides which, had they been told to out fathers, would have seemed little less to them than miracles.

Instead of bees in hives now being carried on a pole between two men (as were those which I first saw brought to my home), we now transport them all over the world by mail and express, altho, as yet, we can hardly say that we send a colony of bees by mail; still the essential part of a colony is thus sent, and I believe that the day is not far distant when enough bees will be sent with a queen by mail to start a colony of bees which will make a "live" of it, if sent early in the season. This will carry our beloved pursuit even to the "uttermost parts of the earth," so that every one can have the privilege of eating honey of their own producing, "under his own vine and fig-tree."

Here, again, we see the working of many minds, for no one man has accomplisht all this; but a little here and a little there has wrought out most of this grand advance during the present generation. The cages first invented for shipping queens would seem bungling affairs to us to-day, yet they had their place in working out this problem—the shipping of queens through the mails.

When queens were first sent by mail it was thought that the apartment made to contain them and their escort must be roomy, so that they should not be crampt, but as time wore on it was found that very little room was needed, and I am convinced that most of the cages now in use are much too large where queens are to be sent by mail with only eight or ten bees to accompany them.

Probably there is no cage in as general use as is the one which is called the "Peet Shipping and Introducing Cage;" yet I firmly believe that the apartment for the bees is much too large in this one. I have used large numbers of these cages, yet I consider them faulty in this respect; nor do I like them as introducing-cages. They are faulty as shipping-cages, in the size of the hole which holds the bees, inasmuch as when the mail-bag is thrown off a train at full speed (as is frequently done), or thrown from the train to the ground, or even from off a wagon, the sudden precipitation of the queen from one side of the cage to the other, often causes an injury from which she never recovers.

The hole in any cage, calculated for holding no more than eight or ten attendant bees with the queen, should not be larger than an inch across the farthest way, and if thus made, the wings and legs of the ten bees will be so close together that they will form springs, as it were, to deaden the effect of any sudden concussion. When thirty or forty bees are placed in a Peet cage, then it answers the purpose of a shipping-cage very well, except that it takes twice the postage that a shipping-cage ought to require, and this matter of postage makes quite an item as regards our profits in these days of close competition, and where queens are sent out by the thousand.

No shipping-cage which meets the requirements as I have set forth can be a successful introducing cage; for to meet with the greatest success in introducing, the cage should cover at least one-sixth of one side of a comb, so that hatching brood and some honey can be enclosed. In the hatching of this brood, to form an escort of bees for the queen, and in her laying eggs in the cells enclosed by the cage, comes an assurance of safety not found in any other item regarding cage-introduction of queens. When these young bees which hatch out with the queen become so attacht to her that they accept her as their mother, it is not long before the bees outside of the cage fall into line. They now begin to feed her such food as is given for egg-production which means safety to any queen. That the Peet cage will not allow of such hatching of bees is wherein it is faulty as an introducing-cage. As the introducing-cage which I prefer has been described in the chapter on introducing laying queens, I will not speak further of it here.

The shipping-cage which I prefer, is made as follows: Get out a block of wood, two-and-one-fourth inches long by one-and-one-eighth inches square. Near one end bore a seven-eighths hole, having the same one inch deep, and boring it across the grain of the wood. In the center of the opposite end bore a one-half inch hole, boring it lengthwise of the grain of the wood, until it comes in contact with the seven-eighths hole which was bored before (Fig. 5, page 35). This last hole is for the candy for the bees to live on during their journey, while the former is for the bees themselves. Next, get a piece of wire-cloth one inch square, and a piece of wood 2¼x1⅛x⅛ inch for a cover to go over the top of the cage after the bees are in and the wire-cloth is nailed on.

The next thing to be done is to prepare the candy for the bees. This is made by taking a quantity of powdered sugar and putting it in any dish; altho I prefer what is known as "Agate Iron-Ware," because in the kneading process, about to be described, the candy does not take on any foreign substance like lead or tin, as it does where a tinned dish is used. If you do not have the Agate dish, an earthen one is equally as good, providing you are careful enough not to break it, thus causing trouble in the family.

Having the sugar in the dish, set the same on the stove or over a lamp, and put some nice, thick honey to heat also (such honey as will not granulate easily being preferred, for spring and fall use), letting both heat slowly till of about the warmth that you can conveniently hold your hand in, when they are to be taken off the fire and some of the honey poured into a little hollow made in the sugar. To get the sugar evenly warmed through, it may be necessary to stir it occasionally.

Having poured in the honey, take a little stick and stir sugar into it by putting the sugar on top of the honey and rolling the whole around. When enough sugar is mixt with the honey so that it will not stick to the hands, when they are rubbed with a little of the sugar, proceed to knead it the same as your wife or mother kneads bread, keeping this up as long as much sugar will be incorporated with the loaf, or until the loaf will not spread out or change its shape if placed on a board.

You need not have any fears that you will get the candy too stiff, for, as a rule, more queens are lost by the candy absorbing dampness, or being left too soft so as to daub the bees, than by all other losses put together. This is the reason for heating the honey and sugar so as to get them of about the consistency they would be in a hot mail-bag during some of the warm weather that we have been shipping queens. This candy is called the "Good" candy, altho that as first made by Mr. I. R. Good, and given to the world, was made without heating, and contained granulated sugar and honey as its ingredients.

Having the candy ready, wet the forefinger of the left hand by touching it to the tongue, when it is to be placed over the one-half inch hole, where the hole terminates on the inside of the cage; when the hole is filled to within one-eighth of an inch with the candy, pressing it in with a plunger.

The wetting of the finger is done so that the candy will not stick to it as it otherwise would do, thus pulling a part of the candy out of the hole, leaving it rough and uneven.

The candy being in place, take a plug-cutter made to cut a one-half inch plug, and cut one out of the one-eighth piece which is to go on the cage for a cover; cutting it out of one end so that the hole where the plug comes out will come over the center of the hole to be occupied by the bees, thus making the ventilating hole in the cover. Now take the plug thus cut and drive it into the hole over the outer end of the candy, when the cage is ready for the bees, all but the wire-cloth.

Put this in place and drive a tack in one corner of it, leaving the tack a little out from the wood, so that the wire-cloth will turn on it, when it is to be turned so as to form an entrance for the queen and attendant bees, which are now to be put in. Place the left hand thumb or fore-finger over this entrance, and with the right hand pick the queen up by both wings and put her into the cage.

If you are not accustomed to this kind of work it will seem very awkward to you. At least it seemed so to me when I first began, so much so that several queens got away instead of going into the cage. To succeed best, go slowly, and see that the queen and bees get their feet hold of the wood, rather than on the wire-cloth, when it will be natural for them to run in instead of backing out.

Having the queen in, close the entrance at once with the thumb, when a bee is to be caught by the wings in the same way and put in with her. Do not raise your thumb off the hole in putting the bees in, but rather give it a rocking motion. As the bee's head nears the hole, rock the thumb back a little, only opening it just enough for the bee to go in, and if the queen attempts to come out, make this bee's head stop the hole at just that instant. Now catch another bee, putting this one in in the same way, and so on until you have enough, when the wire-cloth is to be brought back in place and nailed.

After you get a little used to this work you can put bees into a cage almost as fast as you could peas or beans. If you catch a bee by both wings it is impossible for it to sting you, so that you need have no fears unless you happen to push it against the thumb you have on the cage, in which case you will be quite liable to be stung.

In catching bees to send off with a queen, select those which are from six to ten days old, as nearly as you can get at it; for very young bees, or those that have never left the hive to void their feces, are unfit to send with a queen that is going a long distance, on account of their soiling the queen and cage with the accumulation with which they are filled while passing through the larval and pupal state; while very old bees have not vitality enough to endure a long journey. By a careful watching on your part, as to the development of bees during the first sixteen days of their existence, you will soon know how old a bee is by its appearance.

If the frame the bees are on is jarred a little so as to cause them to fill themselves with honey, they will stand the journey better, and are more easily pickt off the combs, when they have their heads in the cells with their wings standing out.

The bees being in, and the wire-cloth nailed down, next nail on the cover, having the ventilation hole over the wire-cloth; after which you will put on the directions, when it is ready for the mails.

If the bees are put up twelve hours before they are mailed, and left with the face side of the cage downward, but raised a little off the table, the queen will rid herself of eggs, and thus better endure the sudden jars which she will be liable to get.

If the cage has been made according to the foregoing directions, and light, soft wood has been used, the postage required will be but one cent, as it should not weigh more than one ounce after the bees and candy are in. If you send out a thousand queens during the season, the saving in this alone will be $10 over what it would be if your cage required a two-cent postage-stamp; and a saving of $20, if it required a three-cent stamp, as our cages did not long ago. This saving of postage is an item worth looking after, when such saving does not conflict with the safety of the queens.

In all handling of queens, great care should be used not to injure their legs or abdomens. That all do not use this care is evident from the number of queens that I have received minus one or two legs, and often with dents in their abdomens. In putting up bees, don't get excited, and handle them as a "baggage smasher" would a trunk; but keep as cool as possible, and if you find that you are nervous and shaky, put off the caging of them until some other time. I realize that with some I am urging a very difficult matter, for I once knew a man (who came to get some queens that he had ordered) to get more nervous and excited in putting them up than he would have been in fighting with a bear. If you are not used to putting up queens, do not undertake the job when some one is looking on, but go at it alone, when you are in a quiet frame of mind.

CHAPTER XXI.

QUEENS INJURED IN SHIPPING.

Probably there are very few who have received queens from a distance, through the mails and otherwise, that are not aware that some of these queens did not come up to those which they already had, as to prolificness; for such is so common that many of our best breeders have been censured and blamed for sending out poor queens, when they were not to blame at all. Scores of these complaints came to me before I ever reared a queen for sale, and the same has been so general that even Mr. Alley occupies considerable space in his book on queen-rearing regarding this matter.

Now, as a breeder of queens, I suppose that I should let this pass if I would consult my own interests; but I feel that both duty and truth require that I should not pass over the matter without mentioning it. Probably no man in the United States has more flattering testimonials, according to the number of queens shipt, than I have; yet this does not prove that none of the queens that I have sent out have never been injured by shipment. By shipment I include all of the necessary evils attending the removal of a queen from her hive and home, and sending her to another hive and home where she is obliged to suddenly stop a profuse egg-laying, and continue in this condition for from three days to three weeks.

Years ago my attention was called to this matter by some writer of the past, who attributed the trouble to the rough usage to which the queens were subjected in the mails; and gave as a remedy that all queens should be sent by express. In this I thought that I saw an explanation of the unsatisfactory results which I experienced with queens which I had purchast; so for some time after that I ordered all of the queens that I bought sent by express.

However, as I saw little difference in favor of those that came by express, over those which came by mail, I concluded that I must look elsewhere for the trouble.

In studying over the past, to ascertain if I could find out wherein the difficulty lay, I remembered that such a queen, sent me by a noted breeder, had not laid eggs enough during two years to amount to as many as one of my ordinary queens would lay in two months; so I wrote him, asking if he remembered whether the queen was prolific in

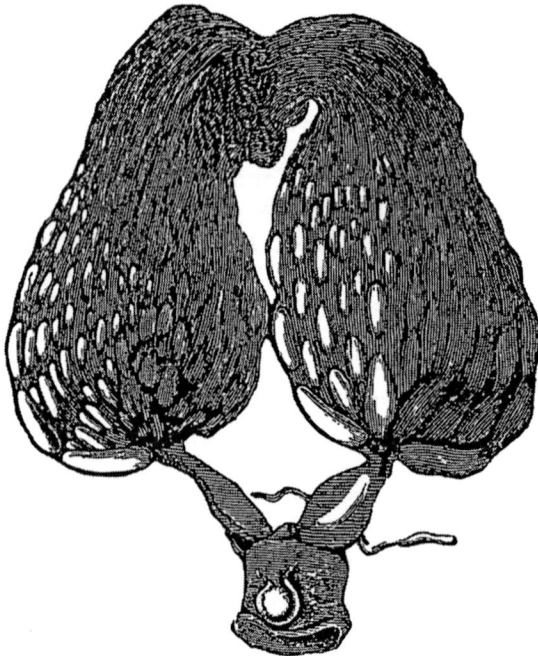

Fig. 12.—Ovaries of the Queen (greatly magnified.)

his apiary or not. His reply was that she was unusually so, and at the time he took her out of the hive she was keeping ten Langstroth frames full of brood.

Later on I received another queen from another noted breeder, for which I paid a very high price, thinking to get the best there was in the country; yet, while she lived, she was about the poorest layer I ever had; still I was assured that she was an extra queen when sent.

Soon after this I commenced to send out queens myself, and during my experience as a breeder and shipper of queens several instances have come under my notice of queens which proved of no special value as to prolificness after they were received by the purchasing party; while I knew that they were among the best, if not the best queens, that I ever owned.

Mr. Alley, in speaking of this matter in his book, attributes the cause to sending off a queen immediately upon her removal from a full colony, while she was filled with eggs; in which state, he claims, she was not capable of enduring the rough usage which she would be subjected to during shipment, and advises that all queens be kept in a nursery for a few days before sending them out. Others have advised leaving the queens caged for a day or two before sending them off; and still others, keeping them in a nucleus for a week or so before mailing them. All of these things show that nearly, if not quite all, of our queen-breeders acknowledge what a few say is not true, as some claim that a queen cannot be injured by ordinary shipment.

While thinking of this matter one day, I resolved that I would find out the truth regarding it, if possible; so I caught some of my most prolific queens and caged them, the same as I would for shipment, giving them the usual number of bees for an escort, and placed them in my shop. A part of these were thrown about the shop, and handled about as I thought they would be when shipt away, while others were handled very carefully or let alone entirely; all being kept from the hive from one to two weeks. Upon returning them as the heads of colonies again, some of them proved of little value, and, strange to say, a part of those that were of the least value were among those treated the most carefully. I was now satisfied that the cause very largely lay where I mistrusted that it did—in the sudden stopping of a queen from prolific egg-laying; for whenever a queen expects to leave a hive with a swarm, she almost, or altogether, stops egg-laying preparatory to leaving, but doing the same gradually.

If I am correct in the above conclusion, and I believe I am, then the plan of keeping queens out of colonies for a week or so before sending them out can only remedy the matter as far as they are liable to being bruised is concerned; while it has really no bearing on the main cause of the trouble. The keeping of them in a nucleus for a few days, would come nearer to nature's way of preparing the queen to leave the hive, than any of the other plans; yet this will not fully accomplish the object, nor do I know of any that will.

Having solved the matter to my satisfaction, that queens were mainly injured by suddenly stopping them from prolific egg-laying, and not finding any plan to fully overcome this difficulty, I next tried to find out if this unprolificness had any effect on the daughters from these once prolific queens, but now almost valueless mothers. I am pleased to be able to go on record as saying, that, so far as I can see, such injured queens produce just as prolific daughters after their confinement as they did before. For this reason I would advise all who receive queens, that do not seem as prolific as they would desire, to rear queens from them immediately, or as soon as any of their brood is old enough for that purpose. In this way the buyer gets a fair return for his money, even if the queen bought does not prove to be all that he had expected or desired.

CHAPTER XXII.

QUALITY OF BEES AND COLOR OF QUEENS.

Had I thought that this book would have been considered complete without it, I should have preferred to leave this chapter out; for I am well aware that we do not all agree as to which is the best race of bees, how these bees should be markt, etc. However, as I thought that all would not consider it complete, and as I desire to injure no one's feelings, I will try in a mild, brief, impartial way to tell what I believe to be the truth about them, as lookt at from the stand-point of this locality—Central New York.

The black, or German bee, probably all are quite familiar with. All the really good qualities that I know of them are their readiness to enter the sections and build comb, and smooth, white capping of the honey of the same. Their poor qualities, as I find them, are their inclination to rob, and willingness to be robbed; their running from the combs, and out of the hive, unless handled very carefully; they do not resist the wax-moths, are poor honey-gatherers, except in times of plenty; are inclined to sting with little provocation, and do not work in a business-like way.

This last particular I do not know that I ever saw mentioned; and by it I mean that they live only from "hand to mouth," as it were, calculating only a day or so in advance. They go into the sections to work, and build comb only so long as honey comes in plentifully. The least slack stops comb-building, only that the cells are lengthened on those that are already built, so that I have frequently found sections one-fourth full of comb, and that one-fourth lengthened out, filled, and capped over, without being attacht to the sections except at the top. I never saw anything of the kind with any other race of bees, for they all start and build the sections full of comb as if they calculated to do something business-like.

If another yield of honey comes in a few days, these bees start the comb down a little further, when it is again stubbed off if the flow slackens; and again and again do the same thing until I have counted as many as five times in a single section where they have started and stopt, making the face side of the comb resemble a wash-board.

It has been claimed that there is a difference in these bees, some saying that there is a large brown bee of superior merit; others claim great things for their gray bees, both of which varieties are said to be a great way ahead of the little black bee; but I wish to say, that, after getting queens from several claiming to have these superior strains, and placing them beside the "little black bee" that our forefathers used to have, there is not a bit of difference in them, so far as I can see, or any of my bee-keeping friends to whom I have shown them.

The queen-bee of the German race seems to be the most constant in color of any of the bees that have come under my notice; all of which are of a very dark brown upon the upper side of the abdomen, while the under side of the same is of a yellowish brown. Out of scores of specimens which I have examined I could not detect the least variation of color, so that in these bees we have queens which will duplicate themselves as to color, if we do not have such in any other race.

Right here I would say, that, in speaking of markings, I shall notice only those which are fixt, or permanent, as are those colors on the horny scales, or segments of the abdomen; for nearly all other markings are of hair or fuzz and are soon worn off, so that an old bee does not look nearly as showy as a young one, when the color of the fuzz is new and bright. The head and thorax of all the races of bees are very much alike, except as the color of this fuzz gives them a lighter or darker appearance. To be sure, the Cyprians have a bright spot, or "shield," as it is called, at the back of the thorax between the wings; but as I find this same spot on the best markt Syrians and Italians, I do not see how it can be used as a test of purity of the Cyprian race, as some claim for it. Hence the abdomen of the bee is the place we are to look for the markings of the different races.

Perhaps I ought not to say anything of the Carniolans, for the two queens which I received that were said to be pure, were not at all alike as to their worker progeny. From these two queens I decided that it was a mixt race, when I lookt at the progeny of one queen; and that it was only a peaceable strain of the black bee, when I handled those of the other queen. My trial of these bees from these two queens, agreed with the reports of the most of those at that time, in that they were not nearly as good as the Italians. As to the "steel blue" color claimed for them, I will say that the same will be seen on a lot of black bees, just hatcht, if held so that the light strikes them just right. From the experience that I have had with these and their offspring, I concluded that I had no use for them, so I superseded the queens. Of late they seem to be growing in favor, and I shall try to give them another trial in the near future.

The few queens which I reared from these mothers varied from a jet black to a light brown, one of which was fairly a shiny-black, like a crow, or what we term a "crow black-bird." There was no constancy of color in either the bees or queens.

I have thoroughly tried the Syrian bees, and for this locality I consider them the poorest of all bees yet brought to this country. The two great faults which make them thus are, first, not breeding when they should breed, and then breeding beyond measure when they ought to breed but little; which results in few laborers in the field in the honey harvest, and countless numbers of consumers after the harvest is past, to consume all that the few gathered. Consequence. no profit.

Second, the workers begin to lay eggs as soon as the queen leaves the hive, whether by swarming or otherwise, so that the combs are filled with a multitude of dwarf-drones, to the disadvantage of the bees, combs, and owner. Laying workers are always present with these bees. At times they sting fearfully; at other times they are nearly as peaceable as Italians. However, they will not venture an attack unless the hive is disturbed, as do the black bees. A colony of Syrian or Cyprian bees will let me stand an hour at a time right in front of their entrance, turning out for me, and not offering to sting; while in less than ten minutes a black colony will resent such impudence to the score of hundreds of stings, if I do not leave.

The Cyprians I disliked to part with, for they were really good bees in all points but one; but that one point was altogether too sharp for me. Of all the bees to sting when provoked, these bees "beat all." In opening a hive, smoke does no good, while the least mishap will, without warning, send hundreds of hissing, angry, stinging bees all over one's person. They also have "a touch" of the laying-worker nuisance, but nothing nearly so bad as the Syrians.

With me, the markings of the Cyprian and Syrian queens are very much alike, except the stripes or rings on the Cyprian queens have more yellow on them than do the Syrians; and the yellow is of a bright orange-color, while that on the Syrians is less bright, and often dusky. Every segment of the abdomen has both yellow and black upon it, unless it be the last one at the tip, which generally is nearly or quite all black, or very dark brown. The queens of these two races of bees are next in constancy of color to the German queens.

Lastly, we have the Italians, and it is hardly necessary for me to say that they are my choice among all the bees that I have ever seen, either for comb honey or for extracted. Some claim that they will not work in the sections readily, while others think that they give the cappings of their honey a watery appearance. In neither of these points do I find any trouble with them; for if rightly managed, so that the hive is filled with brood when the sections are put on, as it should always be, they work in the sections on the first appearance of honey in the fields; while I have none of the watery-appearing honey from them, which is produced by both the Syrians and Cyprians. To be sure, they do not use as much wax on their combs as do the blacks, but they use enough, when we take all things into consideration, such as the cost of wax, toughness of comb, pleasure of eating, etc.

Especially am I pleased with these bees when we have a light yield of honey, for at such times they work right on, untiringly, storing a little honey in the sections every day, at times when hybrids and other bees are scarcely getting a living. They will also work on the red clover more than any other bees, as I have proven during many seasons, storing nice, white honey at the same time the German and hybrid bees are gathering only that of dark color. This one quality alone would give them the preference over the other races, with me, had they not many other redeeming qualities besides.

The queens are very inconstant in color, especially those from an imported mother, such varying from that of a German queen to a bright, golden orange-color the whole length of the abdomen; some of the best specimens of my home-bred stock, not having even a particle of black on the extreme tip, or point. By crossing the best specimens of my home-bred stock, with similar specimens from different apiaries from 100 to 1,000 miles from me, I have succeeded in securing bees of the Italian race which are far more constant in color than any I could get ten years ago; while at the same time my bees have vastly improved as to their working-qualities. By this method of crossing, I believe it possible to get a bee of the highest type, as to working-qualities, as well as to produce the handsomest bees in the world.

While I would by no means sacrifice working-quality for color, or anything else, yet when we can have a beautiful bee combined with one having the very best working-qualities, why not combine pleasure with profit? It is one of the "queer" things which a queen-breeder meets with (as nearly all such breeders will bear me out), that where a party orders several queens, writing that he does not care for color, only give him good working-quality, he will, nine times out of ten, select the very yellowest one you would send him, to breed from, while his next order will call for all yellow ones.

Of hybrid bees I have little to say, for I believe that the crossing of any of the races with those of the same race, procured from some apiary 200 or more miles away, will produce just as good results as to honey, as will the crossing of the different races.

CHAPTER XXIII.

REARING A FEW QUEENS.

No apiarist—no matter how few bees he may keep—should consider that he has done his duty by his "pets" until he has learned how to rear queens. Not only is this a duty which he owes to himself, but in the doing of it he will find the most fascinating part of apiculture. I know of nothing so enticing, or of anything that will so completely absorb the mind, and get one out of that complaining mood which we sometimes fall into, as will the rearing of queens. When at this work, minutes and hours fly away as tho they were not, and even a whole day spent in the closest of this work is only considered a day of recreation. Here we can get away from self and the cares of life, and be led out along a higher plane of thought—thought which grasps, to some degree at least, the mind of our Creator, when He made so many things for the comfort and enjoyment of us, His children. In no one thing can the handiwork of God be seen more than in this particular branch of our beloved pursuit.

Again, the rearing of queens is a duty that we owe to our families, if they are in any way dependent upon us for their support. Many times I see it advised, that the beekeeper should buy his queens, as tho that was the best and cheapest way to Italianize an apiary. While I have queens to sell, yet I object to such advice, or any advice which compels the man starting in apiculture, or already in the same, to take his hard-earned pennies—often earned in some other calling in life—away from his family, and send them for the support of some other man's family who may have many luxuries that his own does not have.

If any one has plenty of money that is hanging idly on his hands, then I have no objection to his sending it when and where he pleases; but I do claim that the average beekeeper has not the right to scrimp his family by buying queens, or anything else, that he can rear or make just as well as not during his leisure moments; and by so doing, keep his money to cheer the hearts of his loved ones, and at the same time be growing intellectually in his chosen pursuit. Of course, it will be necessary for any one desiring a change of stock to get a queen of the desired race, but to purchase queens for the whole apiary, or by the score, as is frequently advised, is quite another thing. The object of this book is to tell all how they can rear one or more queens with ease, and in such a way that their bees can be improving all the while, instead of retrogading, as was often the case where the old plans were used.

But says one: "How can I rear one or two queens by your plan, without going through with all of the work that the plan, as a whole, requires?" If you do not want to rear enough queens to pay for using a stick of twelve cells, proceed to make two or three wax-cups, as I told you how to do in Chapter VII; or, if this is too much work, use embryo queen-cells, as given in Chapter VI. A few days previous to doing this, tier up a hive for extracted honey, as all want at least one hive workt in that way; if not wanted for that, it will be needed for the purpose of securing extra combs of sealed honey, to be used in feeding the bees when they need feeding, putting a queen-excluding honey-board between the hives, and having one frame of unsealed brood iu the upper hive with other combs.

In four or five days, look at this comb having the brood in it, and you will find one or more queen-cells started, from which you can get royal jelly with which to supply the wax-cups that you have made. Just before putting in the royal jelly, go to the hive having your best queen—best as regards color, work and every other quality—and get a piece of comb containing a few larvæ. If the day is not quite warm, take all to the kitchen, where it is always warm just before the noon-day meal; and after putting the royal jelly in the wax-cups, transfer some larvæ into each. Roll the cups in a warm cloth, if the day is cool, and upon going back to where you got the jelly, press down some of the cells a little where the comb is empty, by laying the side and end of the little finger against the comb, thereby forming a place into which the wax-cup will fit nicely, thus holding it in place on the comb with the open end down.

Now put the frame in place in the upper story again, and close the hive. If other cells were started on this comb, besides the ones which you destroyed by taking out the jelly, they should be destroyed also. In case a queen is allowed to hatch from such cells before those hatch which you have started, they will destroy those of a better quality that you have worked for.

In ten days from the time you prepared the cells, go to the hive and slip in a queen-excluding division-board near the center, if you want two queens to hatch and become fertile. If you want only one, you need not fix the hive in this way at all; for the first queen that hatches will destroy all the rest. All you need to do in this case is to bore a half-inch or larger hole in the back part of the hive, five days after the queen is hatcht, and close it again after she begins to lay.

But as it will be natural for you to want two queens at least, we will suppose that you have the queen-excluding division-board in place, after which you are to get a frame containing a little brood, from any hive in the yard, and after shaking the bees off this comb in front of their own hive, you are to take one of the nearly-mature queen-cells off the comb that they are on, and stick it on this comb, the same as you did the wax-cup; using this way of fastening the cells to the comb until you get enough accustomed to the work so that you will not injure them by pressing them into the comb, as I advised in Chapter IX.

Now place this frame on one side of the hive, and the one on which the cells were built, on the other side, having the queen-excluding division-board between them. If you have more than two completed queen-cells, and you wish to save them, of course you will need more upper stories, or will form nuclei for them, this being written on the supposition that you are only desirous of rearing just two extra queens.

In five days after the young queens hatch, bore a hole from the back part of the hive into each of the apartments having the queens, leaving these holes open till the queens begin to lay, when they are to be closed. You will now have two as nice queens as you ever saw, reared without much trouble; and they can be kept where they are until you desire to use them without their interfering with the workings of the colony in the least, any more than they have done so far, which is none at all.

This rearing of queens and having them fertilized in a hive having a laying queen in it, without in the least interfering with the working of the bees or the hive, is something which holds me almost spell-bound when I think of it, and something that we have heretofore considered impossible.

Another point right here (and one which I consider worth much more to any one, than the price of this book, even tho he may keep only two colonies of bees), and that is: If you desire to supersede any queen in your yard, on account of her being too old to be of farther use, or if she is of another race of bees from what you desire, all you have to do is to put on an upper story, with a queen-excluding honey-board under it, place a frame of brood with a queen-cell upon it, in this upper story, and after the young queen has hatcht, withdraw the queen-excluder, and your old queen is superseded without your even having to find her, or having the least bit of time wasted to the colony.

In fact, the possibilities which this perforated-metal may bring, have only just begun to loom up before us, so that what the future may bring forth in this matter can hardly be conceived by any. Truly, our pursuit is one of the most fascinating of any of those that are engaged in by man; and I am thankful to Him who ruleth all things, that I have a part and a lot in this matter.

That all who read this book may try to carry out the

thoughts herein advanced, to still greater perfection, and strive in the future to rear only queens of superior value, so that we may soon be able to say,

"THE COMING BEE IS HERE,"

is the best wish of the author.

CHAPTER XXIV.

LATER EXPERIMENTS IN QUEEN-REARING.

Since writing the preceding Chapters, I have been experimenting further along the ideas contained in Chapter XIII, as I found that owing to the conditions under which I had tested the thoughts and experiments therein contained, there was a possibility of a failure along that line, when the plans were used under other conditions than those which existed during the times when I had formerly used them. In previous years, owing to my selling nearly all of my stronger colonies of bees to fill the many orders which I had for the same, I had no colonies of suitable strength to tier up early in the season, so that the plans then tried were used only after the basswood had blossomed and later, in having queens fertilized over a queen-excluding honey-board. During the next year (1889) having more strong colonies than usual, owing to fewer sales, and the bees wintering better, I tiered up several hives early in the season, and very much to my surprise, found that which had previously workt to perfection was a failure, as far as the fertilizing of the queens from these upper stories was concerned. The cells were allowed to hatch just the same as before, but when the queens came to the age of two or three days, the workers began to worry and tease them, which resulted in their being killed sooner or later, while in one or two instances the result was a general row "upstairs," in which many bees were killed besides the queen. At this time the bees were only living from "hand to mouth," as it were, for the forepart of our season was the poorest I ever knew.

When the basswood began to yield honey, I again

began to have the same success which I formerly had, either owing to the peculiarity of this locality, which brought about former conditions, or to some additions which I made to the hive, or perhaps both. When I saw that what I supposed was the same plan that I had formerly used, was failing, I began to study into the matter to see if I could not find a remedy, and about the first thing which appeared was that I did not have the hive fixt as I had previously, altho I now had it arranged the same as I gave in Chapter XIII in this respect.

Some may think that it would be strange for such a thing to occur, and perhaps it was, yet it was one of the most natural things in the world, as you will soon see. As all of the older readers of the bee-papers are aware, when I commenced using the Gallup hive I used it the same as Gallup recommended, using twelve frames in the hive. As the years past by, I believed that twelve frames were too many for the brood-apartment, so I made dummies or division-boards to take the place of one or more frames, according to the time of the season, or as I wisht to contract or expand the hive, my custom being to expand the hive during the forepart of the season, and contract it the latter part, or contract at the beginning of basswood bloom.

After a little thought along the line of what had caused the failure this season, when no failure had occurred before, it began to dawn upon me that in my former experiments I had contracted the lower hive down to eight frames, so as not to rear a large number of bees during the basswood bloom, to become consumers of the honey later on, as we have no fall flow of honey here; and in this contraction might be found a solution of the problem, for I now had both stories of the hive filled with combs, as it was the forepart of the season, the lower hive being now filled so as to rear workers for the harvest. In this latter case the brood came directly under that part of the queen-excluder running under the apartment petitioned off with the perforated-zinc division-board, so that when the young queen ran down on the zinc, she and the old queen could get their heads together and try to kill one another, which resulted in the bees worrying the young queen when she was old enough to be recognized as a queen, the same as bees always try to worry virgin queens in the queen-nursery after they are two or more days old, as they always do when such nursery is hung in a hive having a laying queen.

When younger than this, the bees do not seem to notice

them in either place, nor does the young queen try to get below. Without intending it, I had so partitioned off the upper story in my previous experiments that the apartments the queens were in, at each side of the hive, came directly over the dummies, so that there was no temptation for the old queen to come out in the bee-space over and between the dummy and the queen-excluding metal, while at the same time there was no brood below these apartments to tempt the virgin queen to try to go below, as there was apparently nothing but wood there; altho the bee-space between the dummy and queen-excluder gave the worker-bees free access up through the bottom of the apartment, as well as through the zinc division-board in the upper story.

When writing Chapter XIII, I had not the remotest idea that these dummies played such an important part in the matter, nor am I now fully certain that they will make the plan a success always in all localities, and at all times of the year, but I believe that they have much to do with the plan working so successfully in this locality; for nothing could work more perfectly than it has with me since the dummies were put in the lower story when fixing the hives for the basswood bloom.

Right here I would say what I forgot to say in the body of the book, which is, that I tack the queen-excluder, used between the upper and lower stories, to the bottom of the upper hive, tacking it on lightly with small wire nails. This makes it so that when I wish to get to the lower hive for any manipulation of the same, all I have to do is to lift off the upper story, the same as would be done were there no queens above, or any queen-excluder used. In this way there is no more danger to the young queens when the hive is off than there is at any other time.

After finding what I believed to be a solution of the former trouble, and knowing that all would not want to use dummies under these queen-rearing apartments, I began to experiment to see how the matter in regard to the young queens going down on the perforated metal, so as to cause trouble, might be obviated, and arrived at the following:

My queen-excluding honey-board is what is called the "wood-and-zinc" board, having a full bee-space on the upper side of it. On this upper side I tackt a strip of wire-cloth of the right width to come out to the queen-excluding division-board, tacking it on each edge of the wood which formed the bee-space, thus giving a bee-space between the honey-board below, and the wire-cloth. which entirely prevented the virgin queen from getting to that part of the queen-excluder immediately under her apartment, yet at the same time allowing the warm air from below to come up into the apartment, the same as it would were the wire-cloth not there.

With this I have been equally successful in having queens mated from these apartments, the same as I was where the dummies were used, and I believe the same will overcome nearly all of the difficulty which I experienced during the forepart of the season, altho I cannot say positively at this date, as I have not had a chance to try it, except during the basswood bloom, and later. If it should not, my next plan would be to make the division, which forms the queen-apartment, or wire-cloth, except say three or four rows of perforated metal at the top, so that all bees entering this apartment would be quite a distance from the reigning queen below, when entering this apartment, which I think would make the plan successful in localities where all else failed.

Now, as there seems to be a chance that a failure may possibly result in some localities, and at some seasons of the year, I would advise all to try only one or two colonies at first, to see if the plan will work in their locality; so that, should it not work, they will be but little labor and time out, in trying to experiment.

I still believe that there is a great future before us, along this plan of having queens fertilized from an upper story, and as I have intimated in other parts of this work, it is my desire that the plans which I have here given may be so improved upon that there shall not be a doubt about this matter, and we as bee-keepers be led out to a wider plain than any heretofore enjoyed.

Already some are branching out along different lines, notably among which is Dr. Tinker, with his "queen-rearing chamber." There is little doubt but what his plan will work, but that "chamber" seems to be more suitable to the large queen-breeder than to the rank-and-file of bee-keepers; while my design was to bring out a plan that would be of benefit to all, from the person having but two colonies up to one who numbered his colonies by thousands.

Some seem to feel (or act as if they so felt) that I was trying to crowd my plans upon them, for some irritation has been shown by a few since this work was publisht; but such is not the case. All are free to use, or refuse, these plans which I have outlined, as they please. No, dear reader, I have not the least desire to crowd anything upon you. All I have done has been done with the hope that I might be of benefit to the world—benefiting some one by smoothing over the rough places a little, the same as some of the writers of the past smoothed the way before my tender feet, when they were still youthful in the pursuit of apiculture.

As I have freely received of the good things in the bee-literature of the past, so I as freely give of the little I know, that I may, in a measure, pay the large debt I owe to those who have preceded me in the way of our delightful pursuit.

Onondaga Co., N. Y., Oct. 1, 1889.

LATEST FEATS IN QUEEN-REARING.

" Scientific Queen-Rearing " cost me five of the best years of my life, as that number of years were given up almost wholly to that work, as far as deep study and experimenting and planning were concerned ; and ten years of work since along that line, without a single failure, with one SINGLE batch of cells, has proved the soundness of what I dug out. Letters have come to me from all over the world, and are still coming, fully equal to those of the first two or three years, telling of the great success obtained by the plans given in the book. This summer I have excelled anything I ever did before. I prepared just ONE colony for cell-rearing the latter part of May ; and this one colony, having a laying queen below all of the time, has reared me a batch of 18 queen-cells every three days ever since, up to the 10th of this month, at which time I started the last batch of cups for this year. I find by my tally-sheet that the average number of cups given each three days was 21, and the average number of queens obtained was 18. So you can see how successful it has been with me during nearly four months in succession. And there are many others who say they do nearly or quite as well. The beauty of the whole thing is, every queen-cell and queen is perfect, and fully equal in every way to those reared during natural swarming, where Nature does her level best. No cells were ever moved from this one colony, from the time the cups were given till the ripe cells were taken away.

Onondaga Co., N. Y.,   G. M. DOOLITTLE.
      Sept. 28, 1898.

* This paragraph appeared in Gleanings for Nov. 15, 1898.—PUBLISHERS.

PRODUCTION

—AND—

CARE OF COMB HONEY.

Upon looking the field all over, I believe I can please the readers no better than by telling them first what I do in my own bee-yard, and how I do it ; thus writing from a practical standpoint rather than trying to theorize, by telling what might be done.

In order to produce good results in comb honey, the first requisite is plenty of bees when the honey harvest arrives, for whatever else we may have, success cannot be obtained without plenty of bees. Again, as I said before, these bees must be on hand in time for the honey harvest, else they become merely consumers instead of producers. How often we find men keeping bees on this (consuming) plan, getting nothing from them in the line of surplus honey, unless it is some little buckwheat honey, or that gathered from fall flowers, which is generally of inferior quality, for the reason that they do not have anything but colonies weak in bees at the time the harvest of white honey occurs. Such bee-keeping does not pay, and for this reason I have dwelt thus long on this part to enable all to see that, of all others, this is the most important item in the production of comb honey.

Our first step, then, is to produce plenty of bees in time for the honey harvest. With most of us white clover is the main honey-producing plant, which blooms about June 15 to 20, and by June 25 is at its best ; hence, our bees must be in readiness at that time if we wish to succeed.

From practical experience I find that it takes about six weeks to build up an ordinary colony in the spring, to where they are ready to produce honey to the best advantage ; so I commence to stimulate brood-rearing about the first of May. I have tried many plans of feeding, both in the open air and in the hive, to stimulate brood-rearing, but finally gave them all up for the following :

When I have decided that it is time to commence active operations for the season, I go to each colony and look them over, clipping all queens' wings that were not clipt the previous season, and equalizing stores so that I know each colony has enough honey to carry them at least two weeks without any fear of starvation. At this time I find, as a rule, each good colony will have brood in four or five combs, the two center combs containing the largest amount. I now reverse the position of these combs of brood, by placing those on the outside in the center of the brood-nest, which brings the combs having the most brood in them on the outside. Thus, while the colony has no more brood than it had before, the queen finds plenty of empty cells in the center of the brood-nest, in combs having some brood in them, and she at once fills these combs with eggs, so that in a few days they will contain more brood than those that were moved to the outside, while the bees have fed and taken care of this as well as tho its position had not been changed. Thus quite a gain has been made in regard to increasing the brood.

In about eight days, if the weather is favorable. the whole yard is gone over again, and this time a frame of honey is taken from the outside of the cluster, and the cappings to the cells broken by passing a knife flat-wise over them, when the brood-nest is separated in the center, and this frame of honey, thus prepared, placed therein.

As I go over the yard each time I am careful to know that each colony has abundant honey to last them at least two weeks, for if we wish to obtain the largest amount of brood possible, the bees must never feel the necessity of feeding the brood sparingly on account of scanty stores. It is also necessary to know that there are no cracks or open places at the top of the hive to let the warm air pass out of the hive, but tuck all up as nicely as you would fix your bed on a cold winter's night.

After seven days more have elapst I again go over the whole yard and insert another frame of honey in the center of the brood-nest prepared as before. If at any time I am short of honey, I use sugar-syrup made by taking confectioners' A sugar and dissolving it in hot water (at the rate of one pound of water to two pounds of sugar), by placing the two in an extractor-can, which should be placed some three or more feet from the floor. Stir well till all is dissolved. Now, procure an old pan of the ordinary size and punch the bottom full of holes about one-sixteenth of an inch in diameter, punching the holes from the inside of the pan, when it should be placed under the faucet to the can containing the syrup. Immediately under the pan place another can if you have it (if not, a wash-tub will answer), and you are ready for business. Take an empty comb and lay it down flat under the pan and on the bottom of the can, when you will open the faucet letting the syrup out in the pan till enough has run out to fill one side of your comb, when you will shut it again.

Turn over your comb and fill the other side, and after hanging in your tin comb basket (wash-boiler, or some convenient tin thing which is almost always at hand) a little while to drain, it is ready to be used in any spot or place, the same as a frame of honey. I prefer this way of feeding to any feeder in existence.

If you wish to make quick work of filling these combs, have an assistant to hand you the empty combs and take the filled ones; roll up your sleeves and hold the combs near the bottom of the can, or low enough down so the falling syrup will force the air out of the cells so they will be filled; turn your faucet so the required amount of syrup will be in the pan all the time, and you can fill them (the combs) almost as fast as he (the assistant) can hand them to you. The sides of the can keep the syrup from spattering about the room, and what is caught therein can be turned into the upper can again.

The next time I go over the yard I generally reverse the brood as at first, as well as to put a frame of honey in the center. By this time the bees will have hatcht out of the combs which were placed on the outside, and as the queen does not lay as readily on the outside of the cluster, these combs will not be as well filled as the center ones.

After about a week more, the yard is gone over again in like manner, and if but nine frames are used to the hive, this time will conclude the stimulating process, for at the end of about five days more, or about June 10, all our frames are full of brood, and our colonies in good condition for receiving the surplus boxes.

MANAGEMENT OF WEAK COLONIES.

Several years ago, when I wisht to unite weak colonies in the spring, I did so early in the season, for the "books" said that the time to unite was when it was discovered that two colonies were too weak to be of use alone, which generally happened in April. That uniting two weak colonies to make one strong one is profitable to the apiarist, no one will deny (unless, perchance, we are obliged to use everything in the shape of bees, as we were in 1882, in order to get our former number back again after a heavy loss); still, that uniting must make the one better than each of the two, would have been when the honey harvest arrives, or our labor of uniting is worse than useless. After practicing the plan given in the "books" for a year or two, I became convinced that colonies thus formed were no better, at the end of two or three weeks, than each one would have been had they been left separate. I have put as high as seven remnants of colonies together, in April, the seven making a good, large colony at the time, and in a month all were dead. After coming to the conclusion that I could not unite bees with profit in the early spring, I adopted the following plan which has proved successful so far :

About the middle of April, some cool evening, I look over all my bees by removing the cap and raising the quilt a little, so that I can see how strong in bees the colonies are, and all that do not occupy five spaces between the combs are markt, and the first warm day are shut on as many combs as they have brood in, and a division-board placed in the hive, so as to contract the hive to suit the size of the colony. Honey enough is provided to keep them amply for two weeks, and the rest of the combs I store away for safe keeping, unless some of the strongest of them are able to protect them from robbers, in which case I leave them outside of the division-board, so that the bees can carry honey from them as they wish. The entrances are contracted so as to let but one bee pass at a time, for the smallest colonies, while the larger ones do not have more than an inch in length of the entrance given them.

The next work is to increase the brood as fast as possible in these small colonies. I keep them shut on the combs first given them till they are filled with brood clear down to the bottom, before they are given more room. As soon as this is accomplisht I give them a comb of honey prepared as before described, placing it between two full combs of brood. In about a week this comb will be filled with brood as full as the others. I go over them once a week in this way till I have five frames of brood in the strongest, when I take a frame of brood just hatching out from those having five full frames, and give it to the next strongest, say, one that has four frames, putting a frame of honey in the place where it came from. Thus, I keep working till all of them contain five frames of brood, which should occur from June 10 to 15 in this locality. I now go to No. 1 and open it, looking the frames over till I find the one the queen is on, when it is set outside, and the four remaining frames and all the adhering bees are taken to No. 2 ; I then spread the five frames in No. 2 apart, so as to set the four frames brought from No. 1 in each alternate space made by spreading the frames in No. 2 ; No. 2 is now closed up, and in a few days it is ready for the boxes. It will eventually make as good a colony for storing in boxes as the best of the stronger ones ; at least such has been my experience so far. I have never known bees to quarrel, nor a queen to be harmed by this plan of uniting, as the bees are so completely mixt up that they do not know what to fight about.

But to return to No. 1, where the queen and frame of brood were left standing outside of the hive. I now place this frame of brood back in the hive and put an empty frame beside it, adjusting the division-board, and I have a nice nucleus from which to get a queen to be used in swarming, as given further on. Many of the old bees carried to No. 2 will return, thus making a strong nucleus, which will fill the empty frame with nice, straight, worker comb in a few days, and still another, if the queen is left long enough.

Now, if I wish no increase of colonies during the season, I serve my whole apiary as I did Nos. 1 and 2, beginning early enough to be sure that none have brood in more than five frames : by putting boxes on the strongest just before apple blossoms, and a few boxes are often filled from this source, as the bees must work in boxes if at all, when shut on five frames. It will be seen that I use nine frames to the hive, but the plan is the same with any number of frames. This having every frame in a hive crowded to the fullest capacity with brood two weeks before the height of the honey harvest, has much to do with a good yield of honey, I assure you. This is the condition I aim to have all my bees in, and I have tried to tell you how, so you can do the same, if you wish to adopt the plan I follow.

GETTING THE BOXES READY AND PUTTING THEM ON.

The getting-ready part I generally work at by odd spells, during the winter and early spring, so as to have all in readiness when they are wanted ; but as this is the time they are wanted, I will give the way I prefer them, and advise that none wait about this getting-ready part till just as the boxes are wanted, because I gave my mode of doing so at the time the bees were ready to receive them. During the leisure hours of winter and early spring is the time to have all in readiness, and they who are not thus ready are often the losers of a good portion of the honey which might be secured.

We have, to-day, two sizes that are generally adopted— the prize box, which is $6\frac{1}{4}$x$5\frac{1}{4}$x2 inches, outside measure, and the $4\frac{1}{4}$x$4\frac{1}{4}$x2, known as the $4\frac{1}{4}$x$4\frac{1}{4}$ section, the one holding about 2 pounds, and the other about 1 pound. The market seems to favor the 1-pound section, not only as to price, but it sells much more readily, and while the prize section goes begging a market, the $4\frac{1}{4}$ is all sold, and more is called for ; therefore, it is easy to see which way the future points as to style of section ; but it is not so easy to see how to change all our equipage adapted to the prize section, and start with the $4\frac{1}{4}$ style without a loss greater than the compensation gained for the first few years at least.

After deciding on the style of section we will use, they are to be filled with comb foundation, if such is thought to be profitable, and if not, put a starter of nice white comb in the top of each box. I prefer to cut these starters in a triangular shape, about 1½ inches long on each side. Now turn your sections top side down, hold a hot iron close to the box, and after holding the starter immediately above and touching the iron, draw the iron out quickly and press the starter gently on to the wood, when it is a fixture. I then fill the cases with sections, putting sections filled with comb left over from the previous season in the center case, if I have them. If I have enough such to fill two cases, I place the two apart so as to set a case having boxes with only starters in them between. When I have enough to do this, I think I am sure of a good crop of honey if such is attainable from the fields, for these combs are more profitable to an apiarist than cash in the bank.

With the brood-chamber filled with brood, as I have shown you it should be, and honey coming in from the fields, these combs are at once occupied, and those sections between and immediately surrounding them, that have starters in, are soon filled with beautiful white comb, and a good yield of comb honey is a certain thing, if the flowers continue to secrete nectar.

Having all prepared, and bees all in readiness, the next thing is to put on the boxes. I generally put on but five cases at first, and if prepared as above, it will be seen that two of these contain sections full of comb, which are ready for the bees to commence work in at once. In about a week all are gone over with again, and if those first put on are being workt in, more are added by spreading those apart, and two more cases are inserted near the center, and by placing a tier at one side. The next time I go over them, probably some will be ready to come off, and in any event as many sections are now given as can be workt in to advantage by the colony, which generally takes the full capacity of the hive.

SWARMING.

After trying all the plans of non-swarming hives given, with no success, I settled down to the conclusion that such a thing did not exist when working for comb honey, and even if it did, I doubt if as large a yield of honey could be obtained, as by the use of swarming hives. Then if we are to use swarming hives, the question coming next is, shall we make our swarms by dividing, or by letting them swarm naturally? Lately I have used both ways with what seemed to me the best results. It will be seen that our bees are all in readiness 15 days before the height of the white clover harvest, and where this is the main dependence for honey, all swarming should be done within the next five days. In this case swarming would have to be done largely by division, but as basswood is my main honey crop, coming about July 5, I do not practice artificial swarming, only so far as is necessary to have all swarming done 10 days before basswood opens. All swarms issuing previous to 15 days before basswood, are hived singly in hives containing frames of empty comb, and in a week from the time of hiving, boxes are put on, in the same manner as described before. Those issuing, the next five days, are hived two swarms in a hive, when convenient to do so, and the full complement of boxes put on at once. If not convenient, the swarm after being hived is set on the stand of another colony which has not swarmed, and such colony changed to a new location, thus securing to the swarm all the field-bees from the colony moved. Each swarm thus made has given them a hive full of empty combs, and the boxes are put on at once. Thus it will be seen all the swarms are in splendid condition to take advantage of the basswood harvest as soon as it commences.

Where I have two swarms together, the queen belonging to one parent colony is allowed to go back, when such hive is moved to a new location and the double swarm set in its place. The colonies losing their queens by their going with the swarms, are allowed to rear their own queens, for (after thoroughly trying the plan) giving each colony a laying queen immediately after swarming, has not proved a success with me.

Eight days after a swarm has issued from a hive I open it, and, having ascertained that a queen has emerged from the cell, by finding one open at the end, I cut off all the rest and thus stop all second swarming. These cells thus cut off are placed in nucleus hives, if I wish more queens. By waiting till the first queen has hatcht, I have a certain thing when the cells are all off, which is not the case where all but one cell is taken away four or five days after swarming; for the bees will often rear queens from the larvæ still in the hive at that time, and also the cell thus left will often fail to hatch.

When I think basswood will open in about 10 days, I proceed to make colonies from all the rest which have not swarmed, as follows: A hive is filled with frames of empty combs and placed upon the stand of one of these colonies which has not swarmed, and all the boxes are taken off and placed thereon, then all the bees are shaken and brusht off their combs of brood and honey, in front of this prepared hive into which they will run as fast as shaken off. Thus I have a colony that is ready for the honey harvest, as they have the queen, bees, and partly-filled boxes all in readiness for work.

Previous to this, nuclei have been started, so that I have plenty of laying queens to use as I need them.

I next take all the combs of brood from which the bees were brusht, except one, arranging them in the hive the bees were shaken out of, and carry them to the stand of another colony which has not swarmed. Next I take the comb of brood which was left out, and go to one of the nuclei, taking out the frame having the laying queen on it, and place the comb of brood in its place. Take the frame, bees, queen, and all, and set it in the place left vacant for it when arranging the combs of brood. Now put on the boxes, and, having all complete, I move the colony to a new stand, and set the prepared hive in its place. Thus I have a laying queen and enough of her own bees to protect her, together with a hive filled with combs of brood and all the field-bees from the removed colony. In a very few days the colonies are ready for the boxes, and generally make the best colonies I have for storing honey. The loss of bees to the removed colony stops the swarming impulse, and in about a week they have so regained their loss that they are ready for the boxes again.

It will be seen my aim has been, in using these several plans, to get all my colonies strong enough to work in the boxes (during the best harvest) to advantage, and still have none of them desire to swarm during the height of the best flow of honey. By adopting a plan called "nucleus swarming," I once had my bees (after an early division) nearly all swarming in the height of the honey-harvest, by which I lost at least $500; for swarm they would in spite of all I could do, and, while the swarming fever is on, but little work will be done in the sections, as all apiarists know. This taught me a lesson; I hope to profit by all such lessons, else why the use of learning them?

HOW TO GET THE LARGEST YIELD OF HONEY.

Having the bees all in, and swarming all done up, the next work is to manipulate the bees and boxes so as to get the largest possible yield from them. Now do not understand that I never have a swarm issue after I have all swarming done (as it should be when the the honey harvest is at its best), for such is not the case. Some of the first swarms will frequently swarm again, or some of those which were moved so as to draw off the old bees, getting populous again, may swarm; but in such instances they are put back where they came from, after extracting every particle of honey from the brood-nest, and cutting out all the queen-cells. Still, as a rule, not many swarms issue after all are prepared as I have described. If a colony is determined to swarm, after this treatment, I generally take off the boxes and put on a second story, filled with empty combs, in which case they will generally go to work with a will. If I cannot make one plan work, I try another. until I strike one that will ; and if a colony is bent on swarming, and will not work in a hive where the lower combs are filled with brood, I take all the brood away. Colonies having the swarming-fever will not do much but swarm, unless some material change is made with the interior of the hive, more than the cutting out of queen-cells; and the sooner this fever is broken up (when it comes during a yield of honey) the better the results. However, but few bother in this way, as most of them settle down to business and stick to it after the swarming proper is over.

After the colonies are all made up, I see that all nuclei have the means of getting a laying queen as speedily as possible ; then I am ready to go over the yard for comb honey. In doing this, I remove the cap and unkey the cases, when they are pried apart a little in the center, blowing in a little smoke to make the bees run out of the way. As the bees clear aside I can see down the flat side of the sections, and, if any are capt down to the bottom, they are ready to come off. If ready, I pry the opposite side of the case loose, when the cases are spread apart a little, and the one having the finisht sections in it is lifted out. I now smoke the bees, to get them off of the brood-combs. They can be nearly all shaken off, except a few behind the separator.

I then take the sections out of the case and place them in boxes which will hold 18 prize sections, or 24 of the 1½ pound sections. These boxes have nails driven in the bottom so as to project one-fourth inch above the bottom of the box, and are so arranged that, by beginning at either side, the nails strike close to the edge of the bottom of the sections, so their weight will keep them prest close to that side, and then they will not be liable to tip over. The object of these boxes are, first, to prevent killing bees, should there be a few not shaken off; secondly, to prevent the sections getting daubed, should any of the combs get bruised, so as to leak honey; and, thirdly, they can be packt nicely on a wheel-barrow so as to be wheeled to and from the honey-house, as well as being handy to carry from the wheel-barrow into the honey-room. Before going to the bee-yard, these boxes are filled with empty sections, having starters all ready for use.

When the full sections are all out of the case, it is filled with empty ones, and put down at the side of the hive, when more are taken in the same way, if any more are ready to come off. After taking all those finisht, the rest are placed close together, and enough partly-filled sections from the sides are raised to the top (by lifting cases, sections and all) till the number wanted is reacht, when the cases filled with empty sections are placed on the sides, in place of those raised to the top, when the hive is closed. I now place a small, flat stone on the top of this hive, that can be seen from any part of the yard, which indicates that I have taken the honey from it. Thus I keep on till the whole yard is gone over.

If the yield of honey is still good, I work in the same way, going over them a week later, except that this time the little stone is taken off and placed beneath the bottom-board of the hive. By using this stone I can see, by glancing over the yard, just how far I have been each time, and the hives which have not been lookt at.

As a rule, when I am ready to go over the yard again, the basswood yield is drawing to a close, so I work accordingly, by narrowing up the surplus room. As the cases are raised from the sides at this time, the follower is moved up, so as to shut the bees out of half the side cases, unless in case of some extremely populous colony, which is treated the same as before. By this means the working-force is thrown into a more compact space, the result of which is a tendency toward completing the sections they have commenced work in, rather than building combs in more. After another week I go over the whole yard again, this time shutting the bees out of the side boxes entirely, which throws the full force of bees into the top boxes, and, altho, the honey season may now be over, by getting this force of bees all together they will cap the partly-filled boxes, where they otherwise would not. This gives sections lighter in weight, but makes much more of our crop in a salable form.

At the end of another week all the white honey is ready to come off the hives, and as a rule my honey harvest is over. In seasons when buckwheat does yield a surplus, I seldom let the bees into the side boxes again, but keep them shut in the top cases.

Thus I have given you the way I proceed to get comb honey. By going over the yard once a week, the honey comes off with a whiteness of comb not attainable when left on the hives till the end of the season, as some do ; and also the bees are kept working to their utmost capacity. Those who think they have a better way of procedure will doubtless think Doolittle does not adopt the best plan to get comb honey. I will simply say that an average of 92 pounds each year, for each colony, for the past nine years, is all I have to recommend this plan,   G. M. DOOLITTLE.

DOOLITTLE'S "ADVERTISING MAN."